FICTION AND THE COLONIAL EXPERIENCE

for V.C.M.

FICTION & THE COLONIAL EXPERIENCE

JEFFREY MEYERS

THE BOYDELL PRESS · IPSWICH · 1973

Published by the Boydell Press
P.O.Box 24, Ipswich IP 1 1JJ, Suffolk.

The following articles from this book have appeared elsewhere:
"The Idea of Morality in 'The Man Who Would Be King,'" *Studies in English Literature,* VIII (Autumn 1968), 711–723.
"Thoughts on 'Without Benefit of Clergy,'" *Kipling Journal,* XXXVI (December 1969), 8–11.
"The Quest for Identity in *Kim,*" *Texas Studies in Literature and Language,* XII (Spring 1970), 101–110.
"Kipling's 'At the End of the Passage,'" *Kipling Journal,* XXXVIII (June 1971), 20–22.
"The Politics of *A Passage to India,*" *Journal of Modern Literature,* I (1971), 329–338.
"Savagery and Civilization in *The Tempest, Robinson Crusoe* and *Heart of Darkness,*" *Conradiana,* II (1970), 171–179.

ISBN 0 8511 5006 3

Printed by Dramrite Printers Ltd., 91 Long Lane, Southwark, London SE1

CONTENTS

It is the spirit of humanity, that which animates both so-called savages and civilized nations, working through a man, and not the man expressing himself, that interests us most. The thought of a so-called savage tribe is generally far more just than that of a single civilized man.

Henry David Thoreau

How far can the civilization England offers be attractive and valuable and be offered and insisted on as an attraction and a thing of value to India for instance? Of course those who live in our civilization and belong to it praise it: it is not hard, as Socrates said, among the Athenians to praise the Athenians, but how will it be represented by critics bent on making the worst of it?

Gerard Manley Hopkins

INTRODUCTION

COLONIAL novels consider the cultural conflict that develops when Europe imposes its manners, customs, religious beliefs and moral values on an indigenous way of life. These novels explore important ideas, for the conflict of ideologies has produced the major crises of the twentieth century; and they form a genre that has an important place in the history of the modern British novel. These novels also consider one of the most significant historical developments in our century, for the tradition of the colonial novel runs parallel to the rise and fall of western colonialism. The colonial genre is virtually invented and introduced into English literature by Kipling in the 1880s, at the apogee of the "scramble for Africa", is improved upon by Conrad, reaches its peak in *A Passage to India*, and is continued by Cary and Greene, who are influenced by Forster and Conrad. After the Second World War, when the British Empire begins to disintegrate, English colonial novels can no longer be a truly vital form and begin to decline.

An analysis of the colonial novel from Kipling to Greene provides a framework for all colonial novels and a standard by which they may be measured. Colonial novels form two large streams, one of them in the tradition of Kipling's early stories,[1] the other deriving from *Kim*, Conrad and Forster.[2] In the first group of romantic-adventure novels, there is no real involvement with the stereotyped native,[3] who is important not as an individual but as an example of what the Englishman must overcome and suppress; nor with the traditional culture or the tropical setting, which merely serves as an exotic background. And the white men are overwhelmingly triumphant against the treacherous and greedy natives, usually with the help of their loyal and self-sacrificing counterparts. The heroes of romantic-adventure novels are physically strong but shallow and uninteresting, and they generally do not learn anything from their adventures. There is a clear distinction in these novels between good and evil, and all moral issues are seen from only one point of view. Everyone who disagrees with the hero is either foolish or evil, and the villain is clearly delineated. There is a vast difference between these adventure novels and the subject of this book: the colonial novels of Kipling, Forster, Conrad, Cary and Greene that seriously deal with questions of cultural conflicts and race relations and offer a valuable humanistic approach to the problems of colonialism.

These novelists find in the tropics a great lure and attraction, a great temptation to atavism, a universal fascination with the savage and the incomprehensible. Kipling yearned for the primeval expanses and felt "If you look long enough across the sands while a voice in your ear is telling you of the half-buried cities, old as old Time, and wholly unvisited . . . [you] will be conscious of a great desire to take one of the lobbing camels and get away into the desert, away from the last touch of Today, to meet the Past face to face."[4] This past can be both psychological and temporal, for in *A Passage to India,* as Stone well observes, "the visitors to the caves are making a return from consciousness to unconsciousness, going back to a prehistoric and prerational condition from which they have been released, but which is still a lurking––though repressed–––presence in them all".[5] Conrad expresses this idea when he writes of primitive Africa, "what thrilled you was just the thought of their humanity––like yours––the thought of your remote kinship with this wild and passionate uproar".[6] For Cary, "The attraction of Africa is that it shows these wars of belief, and the powerful often subconscious motives which underlie them, in the greatest variety and also in very simple forms. Basic obsessions, which in Europe hide themselves under all sorts of decorous scientific or theological or political uniforms, are there seen naked in bold and dramatic action." [7] And Greene writes, "The 'heart of darkness' was common to us. Freud has made us conscious as we have never been before of those ancestral threads which still exist in our unconscious minds to lead us back." In the Liberian jungle, Greene had "the sense that one was nearer than one had ever been to the racial source, to satisfying the desire for an instinctive older gentler way of life, the sense of release, as when in the course of psycho-analysis one uncovers by one's own effort a root, a primal memory".[8]

These passages are remarkably similar. The novelists suggest that by taking the archetypal night journey, by returning to pure nature uninhabited by man, they can also return to a free unconscious state and liberate the repressed primitive element in themselves. They feel that the acquisition of technological civilization has caused serious damage to the human spirit, which can perhaps be redeemed by a temporary return to a more primitive and prelapsarian element.[9]

The tropical colonies provide an extraordinary milieu for human experience. Novels like *The Ambassadors* and *A Room With A View* examine the effect of a foreign country on provincial travellers; but French and Italian culture is essentially similar to English, springs from the same classical source, and is attractive and seductive to foreign visitors. It is only outside the Mediterranean norm that Europeans approach the monstrous and extraordinary.

The deracinated white man in the tropics moves from an ordered to a chaotic world — hostile and inimical, strange and difficult to understand. For beneath the surface lies a stealthy Nemesis, a terrifying, primitive non-culture — variously symbolized as the heart of darkness or the Malabar caves. These symbols represent extraordinary destructive and disintegrating forces that overtake so many of the proud conquering race, and are capable of extinguishing the potent idealism of a sophisticated Kurtz or the benign rationalism of a wise Mrs Moore. The caves and the heart of darkness exist in an environment that is hot, humid, remote, lonely, diseased, dangerous, anarchical, frightening; an environment where all the familiar conventions and meanings are absent, no external restraints are imposed, and the white man struggles with the blind energy of nature, alone, far from the eyes of his fellows; where prejudice and hatred flourish, personal relations disintegrate, and men are overwhelmed, corrupted by power, or annihilated. These conditions provide a supreme test of character, for men must depend on their inner resources and moral strength to meet this challenge and maintain a perilous balance in a world of extremes.

Kipling, Forster, Conrad, Cary and Greene understand the vast potentialities for portraying the dramatic contrasts and tensions of men caught between two civilizations. Their novels evaluate their own civilization and moral standards, and consider two important questions: what happens to the "civilized" white colonist when he is confronted with an alien culture? And what happens to the natives and their culture under colonialism? These questions are of the greatest human interest and are especially relevant in the modern world, for the character's relation to this hostile tropical world often symbolizes modern man's alienation from his own society and civilization.[10] All Europe contributed to the making of Kurtz, who is the prototype of Eliot's hollow men. Lawrence's interest in the Etruscans, Eliot's interest in Hindu philosophy, Pound's interest in Chinese thought, and the exploration of different cultures by Forster, Conrad, Cary and Greene, all reflect a loss of confidence in European civilization and a disillusionment with material progress.

These writers understand that civilization has a destructive as well as a creative power, and are particularly concerned with preserving the integrity of traditional life and culture from what Conrad calls "the material apparatus of perfected civilization which obliterates the individuality of old towns under the stereotyped conveniences of modern life".[11] Forster calls *The Hill of Devi*, a book about his life in an Indian Native State, the "record of a vanished civilisation. Some will rejoice that it has vanished. Others will feel that something precious has been thrown away amongst the rubbish——something which might have been saved." [12] The film *Abyssinia* gave Greene "a vivid sense of something very old, very dusty, very cruel, but something dignified in its dirt and popular in its tyranny and perhaps more worth preserving than the bright slick streamlined civilization which threatens it." [13] And Cary writes, "For even if civilization meant for the Birri a meaner, shallower kind of life, how could any man hope to fight against it when it came with the whole drive of the world behind it, bringing every kind of gaudy toy and easy satisfaction?"[14]

The heroes of colonial novels who must survive this setting and conflict are not like those of epics and romantic-adventure fiction. They are rarely successful or triumphant, have no great physical prowess, and cannot make clear distinctions between good and evil. They usually do not have the stature and depth of a tragic hero, nor his disastrous end. Nor do they have the artist hero's genius and aloofness from the world. These heroes are quiet, defensive, undistinguished, yet sympathetic, cousins to Hans Castorp and Leopold Bloom. They are somewhat disappointing and limited, for they are victims of circumstances they cannot master. They are seriously compromised by the colonial situation, and have an awareness of their own guilt and complicity in it.

These protagonists are moved by the suffering of others and are convinced that man's salvation lies in solidarity. They are deeply involved with the natives and their culture, sympathize with and understand them, and use their imagination to see experience from several viewpoints and to accept the world view of others, as Kim does with the Lama, Fielding with Aziz, Marlow with Kurtz and the African helmsman, Rudbeck with Johnson, and Scobie with Ali and Yusef. For them, the colonial experience is a process of self-questioning and self-discovery from which they emerge with a new self-awareness, heroic in their compassion and understanding. These characters have the keenest perception of cultural differences, but they are able to transcend them to achieve meaningful relationships with men

very different from themselves. Like Fielding, they try to reach other
men with the help of good will, culture and intelligence. The hero's
cultural relativism may lead, as with Fielding, to a fusion of the best
elements of both cultures. It may enable the hero to make a flexible
adjustment to prevailing conditions, to re-evaluate western civilization,
and to strengthen his moral system under the pressure of colonial life.
Kipling's doctrine of work and his idea of the Law, Forster's humanistic
faith and good will, Conrad's concept of fidelity and moral discipline,
Cary's balance between authority and freedom, and Greene's unorthodox
Catholicism are values that sustain men in difficult and intense
conditions.

I

RUDYARD KIPLING:
CODES OF HEROISM

KIPLING'S early stories show his heroes' conflict with the power of India. In "At the End of the Passage" the traditional idea of heroism is too rigid and too constrained, and the would-be hero becomes a victim when his standard of conduct fails to sustain him during a crisis. The protagonists of "The Man Who Would Be King" and "Without Benefit of Clergy" attempt to transcend the traditional code of the white man in India, but are unable to replace it with an alternative moral system of their own. The "kings" fail because they do not possess the moral authority requisite for enlightened imperial rule. In "Without Benefit of Clergy" even powerful love is insufficient to transcend racial differences and the lovers are doomed for breaking the Sahib's code. The hero who is able to cope with the power of India and embrace both cultures does not emerge until Kim, who understands and sympathizes with the Indians, and embodies the best elements of both the Indian and English worlds.

The fascinating thing about Kipling's stories is the difference between their intended and actual effect. He wrote for an audience who accepted his values and agreed with his beliefs, but when we test our ideas against Kipling's we see that his art is sometimes in conflict with his thought. In "At the End of the Passage" he attempts to glorify a code but actually shows how unsatisfactory it is. The theme of "The Man Who Would Be King" is seriously undermined by his glorification of the men he intends to criticize. In "Without Benefit of Clergy" he begins to write a lyrical Indian *Romeo and Juliet* about a love that transcends social differences and ends by punishing the lovers for their racial transgression. And the racial tolerance in *Kim* is undercut by the theme of white superiority. The effect of Kipling's stories is like that of a revolving lighthouse which radiates momentary gleams of revealing light far out into the surrounding gloom, and then suddenly lapses into complete darkness.

1.   "At the End of the Passage"

W. H. Auden writes that, unlike most writers, Kipling is obsessed by a
sense of external, rather than internal dangers threatening civilization.
"For him civilization (and consciousness) is a little citadel of light
surrounded by a great darkness full of malignant forces and only
maintained through the centuries by everlasting vigilance, will-power
and self-sacrifice."[1] "At the End of the Passage" (*Life's Handicap*,
1891), portrays a man whose vigilance and will-power are broken down
and destroyed by these external malignant forces, and who is so
tortured by the powers of darkness that only death can release him
from his hellish existence. Kipling ably describes the destructive power
of India, but is less successful when he writes of the little citadel of
light that opposes it. Kipling's English standards of civilized behaviour,
especially his idea of self-sacrifice, are unsatisfactory and unreliable in
India, and his code of conduct and idea of heroism too rigidly
constrained.

Kipling describes this destructive setting in the opening paragraph:

> Four men, each entitled to 'life, liberty, and the pursuit of
> happiness', sat at a table playing whist. The thermometer marked—
> for them—one hundred and one degrees of heat. The room was
> darkened till it was only just possible to distinguish the pips of
> the cards and the very white faces of the players. A tattered,
> rotten punkah of white-washed calico was puddling the hot air
> and whining dolefully at each stroke. Outside lay gloom of a
> November day in London. There was neither sky, sun, nor
> horizon, — nothing but a brown purple haze of heat. It was as
> though the earth were dying of apoplexy.

This paragraph states the major motifs and dominant images of the
story, evokes the setting and mood with startling vividness and
intensity, and carefully defines what the civilized European must
endure. The physical facts are the most striking. The heavy heat is
terrible, and causes the outside world to become undifferentiated and
unfamiliar when the normal bearings — sun, sky and horizon —
are lost. The image of the apoplectic earth suggests the mode
of death: the loss of sensation and consciousness from brain damage.
The unhealthy pallid faces in the darkened prison, the doleful
whine and the gloom outside, evoke a mood of desolation and
deep despair. The tattered rotten punkah, like the battered little camp-

piano and the miserable goat chops and curried eggs, is a symbol of
their disintegrating and chaotic world. The mention of London recalls
as a frame of reference the civilized and familiar world that the men
unsuccessfully and poignantly strive for. Finally, instead of 'life, liberty
and the pursuit of happiness', Hummil achieves only bondage, despair
and death.

Kipling has rendered the artful *progression d'effet* by revealing how
pitiless and inexorable nature causes physical decay in Hummil, and
how the nervous strain of boredom, anxiety and isolation leads to
spectres and delirium, and causes a fatal relaxation of his moral fibre.
This saps his vitality, enfeebles his will, and forces Hummil to succumb
to panic, terror and madness.

Both Conrad and Kipling write about the disease and madness which
threaten the white man in the tropics, but each has a different
conception of these dangers. Conrad, unlike Kipling, is aware of the
dangers that lie within man — his personal weaknesses and "civilized"
values — that are unable to sustain him in a hostile environment. Conrad
writes in "An Outpost of Progress" that contact

> with primitive nature and primitive man, brings sudden and
> profound trouble into the heart. To the sentiment of being alone
> of one's kind, to the clear perception of the loneliness of one's
> thoughts, of one's sensations—to the negation of the habitual,
> which is safe, there is added the affirmation of the unusual, which
> is dangerous; a suggestion of things vague, uncontrollable, and
> repulsive, whose discomposing intrusion excites the imagination
> and tries the civilized nerves of the foolish and the wise alike.[2]

Each of the four men in "At the End of the Passage" who eagerly
and irritably meet every week is subject to these extraordinary destructive and disintegrating forces, and is thrust into a struggle for existence
in which the weakest succumbs first. Hummil's ghastly death suggests
the fate of the other men just as Jevins' death foreshadows and hastens
Hummil's: for Hummil must add the burden of Jevins' work to his
already strenuous duties. Though one of the ideas in the story seems to
be "judge no man this weather", suicide is condemned not on theological but on occupational grounds: it "is shirking your work". The hazards
and hardships of this work are almost as unendurable as the heat itself.
Lowndes, a political advisor to an Indian Native State, is in constant
danger of being poisoned; Spurstow, a doctor, is threatened by an
epidemic of black cholera; Mottram, the surveyor, suffers from

opthalmia as well as isolation and loneliness. But it is Hummil who
suffers most and, threatened by madness, clings to morphia, the last
appeal of civilization.

Kipling makes clear that these men are living in an earthly Hell,
and as they attempt to sleep in the house of torment they suffer the
cruelties inflicted upon the damned. They endured the foul smell of
kerosene lamps combined with the stench of native tobacco, baked
brick, and dried earth; the punkah flagged, almost ceased, and then
fell apart; a tomtom beat with the steady throb of a brain-fevered
skull; the sweat poured out of the sleepless men; and Hummil, already
half dead, was as rigid as a corpse. After Hummil dies, his servant
explains that his master has descended into the dark places and has
been frightened to death by an unearthly fear.

When Spurstow, who stays with Hummil after the others leave,
realizes Hummil's condition, he urges him to forget his work and wire
to headquarters for leave. But Hummil refuses because he knows his
replacement is physically weak and has a wife and child who would
surely die if they left the cool hills. The camp-piano, the wreckage of
a couple who had once lived in the bungalow, is a warning of the fate
that overtakes families in the Indian heat. Kipling's dedicated men
maintain the tradition of sacrifice to duty, and reveal the terrible
irony in his stories: that the rulers of India often become its victims.

Kipling wisely spares the reader the horrors of the final week of
the victim's life and when Hummil's friends return the following
Sunday they find him dead. The tireless punkah-wallah, who is
unaware that anything unusual has occured and continues to pull the
cord of his punkah, suggests the lack of connection between the
Englishman and the mass of hostile or indifferent natives whom he
attempts to rule.

Hummil's hands are clenched, and the spur that he rested on to
keep him from sleep and tortuous nightmares falls to the ground, a
vivid symbol of how he urged himself, beast-like, to work and to
duty. His friends faithfully return to the work that keeps their wits
together; all that remains is the indignity of hasty disposal, mandatory
in the Indian heat.

The story should have ended here, a powerful tale of terror,
hopeless despair and spiritual disintegration, But Kipling, not satisfied
to rest with this achievement, pushes on to the realm of the supernatural, and nearly destroys the total effect of the story. The very
real horrors — physical, spiritual and mental — were certainly sufficient
to destroy Hummil without the introduction of supernatural elements

(and further unnecessary explanations). The fact that the horrors which killed Hummil remain on his eyes after death and are recorded by a camera adds nothing to the story and is irrelevant to Kipling's intention of showing the self-sacrifice and devotion to duty of these shattered men of imperial fibre.

Kipling fails to recognize that there is something self-defeating about this gladiatorial heroism. He habitually assumes that in such a situation a typical colonial character can behave in one way only, so that Hummil never has a choice to make. There is no possibility in the story of another system of values, no doubt of the inflexible standard of conduct. Kipling believes that Hummil contains within himself all that is needed to survive, and that there is only one kind of manliness and heroism, which is self-dependent and based entirely on will-power. Hummil is intended to be a brave hero and the story is meant to be a tragic defeat of a strong man by a dark colonial fate. The story allows us to imagine an unending succession of martyrs sacrificing themselves to the cause of empire, and shows how completely Kipling believes in the colonial mission.

For these reasons, there is no conflict in Spurstow's mind about his responsibility to Hummil, for the interests of the empire always override those of the individual. Kipling always demands the suppression of the individual, who is important only for his organic value — as a link in the chain or a part of the team.

It is precisely Kipling's assumptions about the nature of civilization, which Auden has observed, that do not allow Hummil to learn from the unhappy example of Jevins, and reveal a fundamental weakness in this and other stories, for the threat to civilization *is* internal. Because Hummil lacks the imagination to see the possibility of acting differently, his rigidity destroys him. What Kipling sees as something external really comes from the rigidity itself. When Hummil must face the power of India, his inner resources and moral strength, his narrow code, his little citadel of light, fail to sustain him, and he succumbs to the doom that waits for "civilized" men at the end of the passage.

2.   *"The Man Who Would Be King"*

"The Man Who Would Be King" (*The Phantom Rickshaw*, 1888), like Shakespeare's *Richard II*, considers the nature of kingship and kingly power, and both works, in different ways, emphasize the human qualities and fallibility of kings who are defeated by their own impetuosity and pride. When Peachey tells the Kafir priest "that the King [Dan] and me are nothing more than two of the finest men that God Almighty ever made. Nothing more, I do assure you," they prosaically and ironically echo Richard's moving and pathetic confession, spoken at a time when kings ruled by divine right:

> For you have but mistook me all this while.
> I live with bread like you, feel want,
> Taste grief, need friends. Subjected thus,
> How can you say to me I am a king? (III, ii, 174—177)

Surely Kipling's epigraph, "Brother to a Prince and fellow to a beggar if he be found worthy," owes something to Richard's

>   Sometimes am I a king,
> Then treasons make me wish myself a beggar,
> And so I am. (V, v, 32—34)

The most important relationship between the two works is that the tragic mood of Richard's "hollow crown" speech dominates the atmosphere of Kipling's story, with all its dreadful forebodings:[3]

> For God's sake let us sit upon the ground
> And tell sad stories of the death of kings—
> How some have been deposed, some slain in war . . .
> All murder'd. For within the hollow crown
> That rounds the mortal temples of a king
> Keeps Death his Court. (III, ii, 155—162)

We only perceive how hollow Dan's crown is when Peachey, crazed like "The Man Who Was", returns with Dan's shrunken head and heavy circlet of gold.

Richard II, the last king to rule by undisputed hereditary right, however deficient he may be in the solid virtues of a ruler, represents a standard of lawful kingship by which Carnehan and Dravot can be measured; and the play provides a touchstone for the characters and themes presented in Kipling's story. Peachey and Dan attempt to transcend the traditional code of the white man in India, but fail as kings because they have no moral standards comparable to the rule of the British Empire and neglect to uphold what Kipling calls the Law — a somewhat vague but important concept that includes fidelity, loyalty, bravery, generosity, discipline, tradition and honour. They are usurpers who bring "Disorder, horror, fear, and mutiny" into the land, "And lay the summer's dust with showers of blood".

Peachey and Dan are uneducated and corrupt adventurers, unscrupulous confidence men, common frauds, blackmailers and drunkards, who have spent most of their fifteen years in India as soldiers[4] and have knocked about in various odd jobs, both legal and illegal, since their release from the Army. Most of their experience is with drill and guns and they use this knowledge to make themselves kings.

Peachey and Dan's kingly ambitions are purely materialistic. They want to "work" the country in order to increase their own personal wealth at the expense of their subjects. They feel that India, if properly exploited, would increase its revenue tenfold. They are desperate men who proclaim the "politics of loaferdom", see economics only in terms of immediate results, and exclude all political, social and cultural considerations. They would substitute economic anarchy for responsible government and replace state control by independent and unbridled exploiters: "The country isn't half worked out because they that governs it won't let you touch it. They spend all their blessed time in governing it, and you can't lift a spade, nor chip a rock, nor look for oil, nor anything like that without all the Government saying, 'Leave it alone and let us govern.' "

In order to free themselves from governmental restraint, the would-be kings go into the unadministered tribal lands. For beyond the frontier "were wild tribes and the Queen's writ did not run. Beyond them again came the Amir of Kabul,[5] but where exactly his jurisdiction ended or began, no one could say."[6] Kafiristan, the eastern province of Afghanistan on the south slopes of the Hindu Kush, is, Dan says, the only "place now in the world that two strong men can *Sar-a-whack*."

Dan's reference is to the northern part of the rich East Indian island of Borneo that became the personal property of James Brooke in 1841. Brooke's motives in undertaking his voyage from England to Borneo were partly love of adventure, and largely the desire to introduce commerce, as well as British ascendency, into Borneo. When Brooke arrived in 1840, a rebellion against the tyrannical officials of the Malay Sultan of Brunei was in progress, and Brooke took an active part in the suppression of this rebellion. As a reward for his valuable assistance, the Sultan made him Rajah and gave him Sarawak, and it prospered and remained in the hands of his descendants until after the Second World War.

Conrad also pays tribute to Brooke on the first page of *The Rescue*:

> Almost in our own day we have seen one of them — a true
> adventurer in his devotion to his impulse — a man of high mind
> and of pure heart, lay the foundation of a flourishing state on
> the ideas of pity and justice. He recognized chivalrously the
> claims of the conquered; he was a disinterested adventurer, and
> the reward of his noble instincts is in the veneration with which
> a strange and faithful race cherish his memory. Misunderstood
> and traduced in life, the glory of his achievement has vindicated
> the purity of his motives.[7]

To Peachey and Dan, however, Rajah Brooke stands for personal
and independent, as opposed to national colonialism, and the absolute
rule of a private individual by force of conquest. When he is encouraged
by his initial triumphs, Dan's vainglorious ambition is to surpass even
Brooke in absolute power, and he ironically proclaims "we shall be
Emperors—Emperors of the Earth! Rajah Brooke will be a suckling
to us."

The "kings" aspire to Brooke's power, titles, wealth and fame,
but cannot support such ambitions with Brooke's genuine concern for
his subjects, his pity, justice, chivalry and nobility. If we compare
Lord Jim, who was partially based on Brooke, with Dravot, we can see
how Jim grows in moral stature, earns the title of Tuan, and assumes,
even unto death, the responsibility for the welfare of his people,
while Dravot does none of these things.

If Brooke was a benevolent despot and a considerable improvement
over his oppressive predecessor, the rule of the "kings", by contrast,
has a disastrous effect on the province, mainly because of their hostility
towards their subjects. Their view of indigenous government as practised
in Indian Native States, for example, is grim. Oppression and crime
are rampant, and the rulers are "drugged, drunk, or diseased from
one end of the year to the other . . . . They are the dark places of the
earth, full of unimaginable cruelty."[8] The "kings" also adhere to the
traditional imperialist view of native history before the English arrived
as one of internecine strife and chaos: "they was fighting one against
the other and were fair sick and tired of it. And when they wasn't
doing that they were fighting with the Mohammedans."[9]

The adventurer's view of the natives is that they are meant to fight
with, conquer and rule. The natives are expendable, inferior to the
white man, easily dominated, and gullible — for after their forceful

conquest, as Dravot realizes, "They think we're Gods." Like Kipling, the "kings" associate right with might, and believe that the white race is superior and has a right to dominate "inferior" ones. They do not recognize that the hill tribes may have a viable life and culture of their own[10] ("Dravot he goes to the biggest [native] . . . rubbing his nose respectful with his own nose, patting him on the head"), and assume that their rule would be better than what the natives had before. Because there is no cultural dialectic or recognition of cultural values other than the most debased English ones, the relationship of the English and the natives is expressed purely in terms of brute force and military conquest.

The methods that the "kings" use to subvert the rulers and subdue these lesser, albeit Aryan breeds ("Boil 'em once or twice in hot water, and they'll come as fair as chicken and ham") is the traditional imperialist *divide et impera*. They side with one of the tribes and overwhelm the poorly armed opposition by means of the vastly superior fire power of their Martini rifles, which keeps them beyond the range of their enemy's weapons:

> ten men with bows and arrows ran down that valley, chasing twenty men with bows and arrows, and the row was tremenjus. . . Says Dravot, unpacking the guns — 'This is the beginning of the business. We'll fight for the ten men,' and with that he fires two rifles at the twenty men, and drops one of them at two hundred yards from the rock where he was sitting. The other men began to run, but Carnehan and Dravot sits on the boxes picking them off at all ranges, up and down the valley. Then we goes up to the ten men that had run across the snow too, and they fires a footy [worthless] little arrow at us. Dravot shoots above their heads and they all falls down flat. Then he walks over and kicks them.

Peachey and Dan consider this battle to be a notable military exploit, and fail to recognize how easy their conquest was and how limited their glory.[11]

Such calculated and brutal forms of conquest, combined with an insatiable desire to rob the land of its wealth, represent the very worst kind of colonialism. Peachey and Dan embody what Kipling has called "No law except the sword/ Unsheathed and uncontrolled",[12] and they prove Lord Acton's maxim that "power tends to corrupt; and absolute power corrupts absolutely." The rapacity of the "kings" for the gold that lies in the rocks, the turquoise in the cliffs, the garnets in the sands of the river, and the chunks of amber recalls Edmund Burke's eloquent condemnation of the East India Company in 1783: "animated with all the avarice of age and all the impetuosity of youth, they roll in one after another, wave after wave; and there is nothing before the eyes of the native but an endless, hopeless prospect of new flights of birds of prey and passage, with appetites continually renewing for a food that is continually wasting."[13]

In both *Victory* and *Heart of Darkness* Conrad also attacked colonialism and "these white men [who] looked on native life as a mere play of shadows. A play of shadows the dominant race could walk through unaffected and disregarded in the pursuit of its incomprehensible aims and needs."[14] The aims of Peachey and Dan are like those of Kurtz and the Eldorado Exploring Expedition, a lust for wealth completely without moral purpose. But the moral awareness that redeems Kurtz in Marlow's eyes, despite his descent into bestiality and corruption, is totally lacking in Carnehan and Dravot.

It was not, of course, Kipling's intention to attack colonialism as Burke and Conrad did, but rather, to present an example of imperialistic control devoid of all moral authority. The story of Carnehan and Dravot represents the dangers and horrors that would result if the organized governments of civilized powers refused the task of colonialism. Hobson quotes his opponents' familiar argument for responsible colonialism, which is very close to Kipling's theme in this story and also describes with remarkable exactness and accuracy the reprehensible actions of the exploiters:

> a horde of private adventurers, slavers, piratical traders, treasure hunters, concession mongers, who, animated by mere greed of gold or power, would set about the work of exploitation under no public control and with no regard to the future, playing havoc with the political, economic, and moral institutions of the peoples, instilling civilised vices and civilised diseases, importing spirits and firearms as the trade of readiest acceptance, fostering internecine strife for their own political and industrial purposes, and even setting up private despotisms sustained by organized armed forces.[15]

Though Peachey and Dan are private despots, they are not entirely lacking a code of moral restraint, which, in so far as they have any at all, is embodied in their "Contrack". This "Contrack" is a magnificent example of elaborate form and insubstantial content, a ridiculous and mock-heroic statement of self-encouragement, and a revelation of the weaknesses that will cause their downfall:

> This Contract between me and you pursuing witnesseth in the name of God—Amen and so forth.
> (One) That me and you will settle this matter together: i.e. to be Kings of Kafiristan.
> (Two) That you and me will not, while this matter is being settled, look at any Liquor, nor any Woman, black, white or brown, so as to get mixed up with one or the other harmful.
> (Three) That we conduct ourselves with dignity and discretion and if one of us gets into trouble the other will stay by him.

This grandiloquent and ungrammatical "Contrack" is clearly derived from the one Tom and Huck signed in the tenth chapter of *Tom Sawyer:* "Huck Finn and Tom Sawyer swears they will keep mum about this [Injun Joe] and they wish they may drop down dead in their tracks if they ever tell and rot." Huck and Tom do "keep mum" and remain faithful to their oath sealed in blood, while Peachey and Dan, who in many respects are grown-up versions of Huck and Tom, break their "Contrack".[16] Kipling's boyish love of adventure for its own sake helps to explain why he minimizes the brutality of Peachey and Dan in favour of their daring. The "kings" have the true stuff of Empire builders, but lack the moral restraint of the Law.

Peachey and Dan must be judged, ultimately, not only by their aims and methods of conquest, but also by the nature of their kingship. Both Brooks and Warren, and Fussell, in the two most careful considerations of this story, admire the kings. Brooks and Warren state rather warily,

> There is a growing sense of responsibility for, and pride in, the people that they rule. Dravot begins to talk about bringing in skilled administrators, recognizing with an unexpected kind of humility that the business of kingship is more complicated than he had thought. He even begins to dream of turning his kingdom over to Queen Victoria — of taking his place in history as one of the Empire builders.[17]

But this statement begs the question of Dravot as king. Dan may "begin to talk about" and "begin to dream of" doing positive and beneficial things, but the only things he actually does, apart from killing the people and looting the land, are bring in guns and repair the bridges, the usual accomplishments of fascist dictators.

The "kings' " pride in their people is dubious, for they merely use them as tools for their own ends, and wantonly attack and kill their own defenceless men in the same way they once killed their enemies.[18] When they first conquer the land "Carnehan sights for the brown of the men" and fires "into the brown of the enemy". When Dan is bitten and bleeds, he "fired into the brown of 'em with an English Martini and drilled three beggars in a line." Peachey and Dan view the undifferentiated brown natives as cannon fodder and unworthy recipients of the white man's bullets. Dravot's kingship is based only on power and fear, for once his mortality is exposed, his most loyal followers attack him. As for the skilled administrators, "to help us govern a bit", Dan intends to bring in his old cronies, the flotsam and jetsam of British India, men as unworthy and unfit to rule as he is: "Mackray, Sergeant-pensioner of Segowli — many's the good dinner he's given me, and his wife a pair of trousers. There's Donkin, the Warder of Tounghoo Jail".

The central speech of the story to which Brooks and Warren refer, " 'I won't make a Nation,' says he. 'I'll make an Empire!. . . I'll treat with the Viceroy on equal terms,' " is not, as Fussell claims, "Kipling's delighted mimicry of the standard British imperialistic posture,"[19] but, through deliberate exaggeration and comic irony, a revelation of how a glorious ideal sounds when presented by an unworthy man. The "imperialistic posture" is one that Kipling himself frequently and seriously assumed . In "Ave Imperatrix" Kipling proclaimed,

> And all are bred to do your will
> By land and sea — wherever flies
> The Flag, to fight and follow still,
> And work your Empire's destinies.

This divine right of colonists was sustained by the idea of progress, European cultural superiority and ethnocentric nationalism, the most characteristic ideas of Victorian England, and was popularized principally by Kipling and by his mentor Carlyle. Carlyle wrote that "two tasks disclose themselves: the grand industrial task of conquering some half or more of this Terraqueous Planet for the use of man; then secondly, the grand Constitutional task of sharing, in some pacific endurable manner, the fruit of said conquest, and showing all people how it might be done." "Sugar Islands, Spice Islands, Indias, Canadas, these, by the real decree of heaven, were ours."[20] This religious conception of Empire is reflected in the "kings' " frequent reference to the Bible, in their assumption of godlike qualities, in their plan of sending "twelve picked English" 'Apostles' to treat with the Viceroy, in the identification of Peachey with Christ (the "Son of Man") in the closing hymn, and finally in the crucifixion of Peachey. But the Christ symbolism is wantonly thrust upon Peachey and fails artistically because he is no more like Christ than the heathens of Kafiristan. Many of his actions, like pagan blood sacrifice, blasphemy and murder, are a complete repudiation of Christian principles. Peachey's crucifixion, like the early reference to a Rajah beating his mother to death and the decapitation of Dan, reveal only the "unimaginable cruelty" of the natives, and Kipling's predilection for horrible details.[21]

Freemasonry, like the "Contrack," provides another system of values in this story, but it is as specious and false as the "kings'" version of Christianity. Freemasonry intrudes unduly in the story, and diminishes its credibility. The incident of the mark on the stone, for example, is childish and trivial. Fussell, who seems to have accepted Kipling's evaluation of Freemasonry, writes unconvincingly that the elements of Freemasonry that influence the story are "its emphasis on universal brotherhood; its search for the common element in mankind; its disinclination to quarrel over politics and religion."[22] On the contrary, none of these elements is reflected either in this story or in Kipling's other writings which, in fact, betray these principles. The craft really confirms caste by allowing a temporary lapse into democracy while the Lodge is in progress; and it shows the same hierarchy, rigid ranking and subordination of men that Kipling so much admired in the public school and the Army. Peachey and Dan merely use Freemasonry as another means of tricking the natives and gaining power. Their godlike relation to the natives, whom they slaughter indiscriminately, can hardly be called one of "universal brotherhood". Rather than manifesting a "disinclination to quarrel over politics," the "kings" simply kill any natives who oppose them.

Finally, we must consider what kind of heroes Peachey and Dan are, unrestrained by their "Contrack", Christianity or traditional Freemasonry. Brooks and Warren write of Dravot, "it is he who rises to the heroic gesture at the end and who dies like a king. Yet one could at least argue that this is Peachey's story since he too learns the nature of kingship through witnessing Dravot's heroic action, and since, magnificently loyal to the memory of Dravot, he acts out a heroic role himself."[23] And Fussell agrees that "Dravot performs the act of magnanimous personal sacrifice by which *alone* kingship is to be defined."[24] When Dan volunteers "I'll go and meet 'em alone" and dies "like a gentleman", it is a "heroic gesture" but not genuine and sustained heroism. If there is any sacrifice involved, it is for Peachey and not for his people (many of whom have been killed on his account), and surely his attitude toward his subjects is another valid and essential way to define kingship.

Though Kipling's theme is the need for moral authority represented by the law of the British Empire,[25] he fails to maintain a consistent moral perspective in the story. Kipling's portrayal of Dan's bravery and Peachey's martyrdom shows his sympathy for the roguish and daring aspects of their personalities. This obscures the moral issue of their behaviour as "kings" — their greed, exploitation, despotism and murder — that he is trying to criticize. Their terrible deaths, which should have been a just punishment for their crimes, become instead an attempt to vindicate their character. The serious flaw of this story is that Kipling is essentially sympathetic to their imperialistic ambitions (that is, the need to replace native anarchy with British order),[26] so that his criticism of their failure to establish progressive beneficent rule and their lack of fidelity to the Law is never forcefully established.

3.   *"Without Benefit of Clergy"*

The tender love of Ameera and Holden, which in the early part of "Without Benefit of Clergy" (*Life's Handicap*, 1891) appears to be so beautiful and perfect, and which reaches its apotheosis in the wonderfully lyrical nocturne as they sit by the low white parapet of the roof, overlooking the city and its lights, is unable to transcend their racial differences and successfully fuse both cultures. Gilbert surely misinterprets the story when he states, "In the last analysis the title represents Kipling's approval of the couple, of their life together."[27] On the contrary, their union is destroyed by cultural conflicts, both internal and external, which find expression in the doubts, anxieties and fears of the lovers, who suffer the visitation of fever, cholera and finally the physical destruction and total annihilation of their house as a fatal retribution for breaking every rule and law of the white man's code. Their love becomes all the more poignant when it is viewed as a brief and pathetic interlude before the inevitable punishment. Though Ameera and Holden have been happily "married," albeit without benefit of clergy, ceremony or church, for two years when the story opens, Ameera is afraid of losing Holden. "How could I be sure of thy love," she asks Holden in the first lines, "when I knew that I had been bought with silver?" She is joyous about the birth of her son, not only for the usual reasons, but also because she (and her mother) feel her son will bind her elusive and shadowy husband to her. One of the many ironies of the story is that the birth and sudden death of their son, the living embodiment of their union whose body unites the blood of the two races, marks the beginning of their doom.

Ameera also fears "the *mem-log* — the white women of thy own blood" who enjoy "benefit of clergy" in the sacramental as well as in the penal sense. It seems to Ameera that these privileged beings unjustly postpone the punishment of death and live for three times the length of her life. The white women escape death because they have the "benefit" of spending the unhealthy hot season in the hills, which Ameera refuses to have, for her love for Holden seems greater and stronger than that of any white women in Kipling's stories. "How shall I depart," Ameera asks, "when I know that if evil befall thee by the breadth of so much as my littlest finger-nail — is that not small? — I should be aware of it though I were in paradise?"

When Ameera tells Holden he has made her very English, she is speaking more truth than she realizes. This does not mean she has become anglicized like the bold white *mem-log*, but that she has completely accepted the English attitude towards miscegenation. She succumbs to the idea of white superiority (this is why she is so fearful) and repeatedly tells Holden she is his servant and his slave, and would not have it otherwise. Her highest aspiration for her son is that he be, not a pundit, but a trooper of the Queen, since half-castes are barred from the officer class. What is for Holden merely a nursery-rhyme whim ("And if it be a boy he shall fight for his king"), is for Ameera a very real hope. When she is on her deathbed, as the first drops of rain bring shouts of joy in the parched city, Holden is transformed in her mind from absolute master into a divine god whom she alone worships and who replaces even Allah Himself. Her last words are a blasphemous variation of the traditional Islamic affirmation of faith, which she had whispered into her son's ear just after he was born: "I bear witness that there is no God but God" (*La Ilaha Illallah*).

She now distorts this into "I bear witness . . . that there is no God but—
,thee, beloved."

Unlike the English who are married in church and hope to be
reunited after death, Ameera believes their religions will keep them
apart after life as they did in life, and that they will be taken to strange
and separate paradises. Perhaps this is why her grief overwhelms her
love when her son dies, and she screams her regrets at Holden: "The
white men have hearts of stone and souls of iron. Oh, that I had married
a man of mine own people — though he beat me — and had never
eaten the bread of an alien."

Ameera's anxieties and fears are also shared by Holden who
constantly anticipates Ameera's death, and has a foreboding of the
inevitable doom that threatens his uneasy love. After his son is born
he is filled with a dread of loss, and when the cholera comes he is
absolutely certain Ameera will die. This dread and absolute certainty
stem from his need to expiate the guilt he has incurred by breaking
the Sahib's code and living with a native woman.

Holden seems to have acquired from Ameera a great deal of Moslem
fatalism. This is inevitable when there is extremely high infant
mortality and continuous epidemics, when the dead cart bears the
corpses through the city gate each morning, when they are separated
for twelve hours each day and she might die in three, and when the
rains instantly turn dust into torrents of mud and scour open the
shallow graves. With resolute acceptance of her fate, Ameera exclaims
of her son's death, "It was written." And Holden's butler, Ahmed Khan,
who like all Indians has known much suffering, intuits Holden's grief
and says, "The shadows come and go, sahib; the shadows come and go."
Holden learns only too well to touch happiness with caution and to
snatch joy under the shadow of the sword that takes life suddenly and
without warning.

Just as Ameera has acquired certain English ways of thinking, so
Holden has learned Moslem customs. When the watchman Pir Khan
suggests a birth sacrifice to guard the newborn child from an evil fate,
Holden decapitates the goats and mutters the Moslem prayer while
raw blood spurts over his riding boots. Like the dagger laid on the
threshold of the baby's room to avert ill luck, which Holden breaks
with his heel, the birth sacrifice is unable to prevent the child's death.
These Moslem customs are ultimately meaningless and cannot unify
Holden's "double life". The discordance of his two lives is symbolized
when the men in the Club are upset by the blood on his boots.

These bloody boots suggest the conflict between life with Ameera and the work, orders and duty which take Holden from her. There is a recurrent heaven-hell contrast between his dark empty bungalow and the Club where Holden must repress his emotions and hide all trace of his happiness; and his sleeping baby, the gentle bullocks, the croaking water pipe, the spinning, the music and the moonlight of the peaceful courtyard where he expresses his tenderness, joy and love. But when the child and Ameera die, these worlds are reversed. The peaceful courtyard becomes a hell of self-questioning reproach and work a welcome distraction from grief and despair. Kipling's men court disaster and tragedy when they commit themselves to love instead of work.

The destruction of love between English and Indian is also found in several earlier stories. The more didactic and less successful tales like "Lispeth" and "Beyond the Pale" (both 1888), in which there is a forceful statement of the "rules" and the "law," and a harsh punishment for those that transgress them,[28] are a faithful reflection of contemporary racial attitudes which, as Spear notes, had changed considerably since the English first established their domination of India after Clive's victory over the French at Plassey in 1757.

> There was no very lasting colour prejudice in the early eighteenth century, and marriage with coloured women was accepted as the normal course[29] ... [but] as the century drew to its close, a change in the social atmosphere gradually came about. The frequency of grand dinners and "reciprocal entertainments" decreased, the formation of intimate friendship with Indians ceased. . . . The higher posts of the Government were filled with appointments from England, its designs became more imperial and its attitudes more haughty and aloof . . . . A "superiority complex" was forming which regarded India not only as a country whose institutions were bad and people corrupted, but one which was by its nature incapable of ever becoming any better.[30]

The theme of "Lispeth" is that "it was wrong and improper of Lispeth to think of marriage with an Englishman, who was of a superior clay."[31] When the missionaries who converted Lispeth lie to her about the possibility of marriage and she is jilted by the white man whom she had nursed to health, she returns to her own "savage" people, marries a peasant who beats her, and soon loses her beauty. Kipling is neither willing to permit Indians to marry whites nor to allow Indians a viable emotional and cultural life of their own. Wife-beating is the *sine qua non* of his native marriages.

When he courts Bisesa, Trejago goes "Beyond the Pale" of white people and beyond the realm of white law, for as Kipling emphatically states, "A man should, whatever happens, keep his own caste, race and breed. Let the White go to the White and the Black to the Black."[32] Bisesa's punishment for Trejago's transgression is much more violent and brutal than Lispeth's. When Trejago visits her some weeks later, both her hands have been cut off at the wrists. It is always the Indians who are punished, never the English; and Gilbert is quite mistaken when he writes of "Without Benefit of Clergy", "When death comes at last, it is merely another random accident, without moral significance. Holden might just as easily have died in Ameera's place".[33] The degree of English involvement with Indian suffering indicates the emotional depth and force of the story. In "Lispeth" the Englishman is unaware of her beatings; in "Beyond the Pale", Trejago is shocked by the mutilation; and in "Without Benefit of Clergy" Holden is shattered by Ameera's death.

The last story is one of Kipling's best, though it is seriously flawed. The intrusion of the ubiquitous Member for Lower Tooting is aesthetically unsound. The cruelty of the old mother who "would have sold Ameera shrieking to the Prince of Darkness if the price had been sufficient" (Ameera's fate could not have been much worse if she *had* been sold to the devil), and her rapacity for the house-fittings that make her forget to mourn her daughter's death, are entirely gratuitous. Her relationship to the gentle and kind Ameera does not seem credible, and she is much more in keeping with the intended mood of the story when she is spinning in the lower verandah. Despite some moments of tenderness and pathos, Kipling tends to express human emotions in banal and unconvincing physiological terms. The baby's cry "sent all the blood into the apple of his [Holden's] throat", the child's tenderness "made him choke" and a tale of cholera made his "blood run cold". The story gives fair promise of examining interracial love and the relationship between Holden and Ameera is sensitively established, but the violent destruction of their love before it has a chance to mature makes it seem almost unreal.

Like Carnehan and Dravot, Holden attempts to transcend the white man's code, but is unable to replace it with an alternative moral system of his own. There is an acknowledgment of shame and guilt in the way he accedes to the imperious necessity for hiding all trace of his powerful love for Ameera. The marriage is doomed to destruction, not by fever and cholera, but rather by Kipling's sanction of the "colour prejudice" and "superiority complex" of his age. The final irony is that Ameera's greatest fear may well come to pass as she had predicted: "When I die, or the child dies, what is thy fate? Living, thou wilt return to the bold white *mem-log*, for kind calls to kind."

4. *Kim*

The most remarkable thing about *Kim* is Kipling's unusual sympathy for Indian characters, customs and cultures. With the sole exception of "The Miracle of Purgan Bhagat" *(The Second Jungle Book,* 1894), a story of a successful Brahmin who retires from the active world to live the meditative life of a holy man, *Kim* is, in tolerance and gentleness, quite unlike Kipling's previous works. The early stories are based on immediate and actual experience, while *Kim* (1901) was written ten years after Kipling's last visit to India when he was a mature and famous writer with a well-established reputation. This novel evolves from a highly idealized remembrance of things past that reaches far beyond the arrogant and satirical tales of his youth to his profound childhood love of India and its people. Kipling's lines on India in his auto-biography, *Something of Myself* (1937),

> Try as he will, no man wholly breaks loose
> From his first love, no matter who she be,[34]

suggest the strength of his childhood attachment to India. Kipling tells us that like Kim, he spoke the vernacular as a child, and he nostalgically remembers "Meeta, my Hindu bearer, [who] would sometimes go into little Hindu temples where, being below the age of caste, I held his hand and looked at the dimly-seen, friendly gods."[35]

But in the 1880s when Kipling first began to write, race relations in India were at their worst, and had been aggravated by the Cowan episode of 1872 in which forty-nine Indians were illegally bound to guns and blown apart; the Ilbert Bill of 1883, that proposed that Indian magistrates be allowed to try Europeans and caused an irrational and hysterical outburst of racial hatred; and the formation in 1885 of the nationalist Indian Congress Party. Racial arrogance was more widespread than at any time before or since. The young Kipling, born in India, with a public school but not a university education, physically unattractive, unusually dark, extremely nearsighted, person-ally insecure, unknown and aggressively trying to make his way in the

world, felt threatened by India and the Indians and easily succumbed
to this strong racial prejudice.

Woodruff helps to explain why the *bêtes noires* of the younger
Kipling were the Bengali *babus* whom he always portrayed as cowardly,
contemptible, unctuous and ridiculous.

> Instead of turning Christian or utilitarian, nationalism turned
> defiantly Hindu. And more and more educated Indians were in
> varying degrees nationalist at heart. They were rivals for power
> and knowledge, sharp critics too of all that Western world in
> which they claimed a share, and it was easy to be jealous and
> resentful of them, to fall into the habit of glorifying instead the
> villager, the soldier, the servant, all who had not yet been "spoilt
> by education", who were still ready to use the old obsequious
> expressions of respect.[36]

In "The Head of the District" (*Life's Handicap*, 1891), for example,
the Bengali *babu* Grish Chunder Dé, M.A. succeeds an Englishman who
has just died of fever, runs during the first crisis, and causes disaster.
In *Kim*, however, Hurree Chunder Mookerjee has no nationalistic
aspirations and desires only to serve the English and become a Fellow
of the Royal Society through his ethnological work. Kipling's sympathetic portrayal of the *babu* is a complete *volte-face*, not only from
"The Head of the District", but also from his early poem "Hurree
Chunder Mookerjee, Pride of Bow Basar", where the same Hurree is
portrayed as a fool and a coward. It is ironic that the Russian and
French spies' incorrect interpretation of Hurree's character is uncomfortably close to Kipling's usual portrait of *babus*.

> "He represents *in petto* India in transition — the monstrous
> hybridism of East and West," the Russian replied. "It is *we* who
> can deal with Orientals."
> "He has lost his own country and has not acquired any other.
> But he has a most complete hatred of his conquerors."[37]

Another native character, the Pathan Mahbub Ali, is an Afghan like
the Kafirs whom Peachey and Dan so indiscriminately slaughter.
Kipling usually portrays Afghans as bloodthirsty savages who gain his
grudging admiration for their ferocity and bravery in battle.[38] But
when Mahbub's useful talents are placed in the service of the English,
Kipling's admiration, like Kim's, is unqualified.

The two clergymen in *Kim* are judged by their attitude toward the Indians. The unpleasant Mr Bennett who loses Kim to the sympathetic Father Victor states, "My experience is that one can never fathom the Oriental mind"(90). This is very close to what Kipling wrote in "One Viceroy Resigns." (1886):

> You'll never plumb the Oriental mind
> And if you did, it isn't worth the toil,

and reveals a sharp change of attitude in *Kim*.

Another striking difference between *Kim* and the earlier stories is in Kipling's use of setting. Born and nurtured in India, Kim knows the land and the customs of the land. He is at one with the Indian setting and moves easily and comfortably in it, whether it be the housetops and back alleys of Lahore, the Kashmir Serai, the wonders of the multifarious Great Trunk Road, the fantastic buildings of garish Lucknow, or the placidity and grandeurs of the Himalayan heights. India is, as Kim says, all pure delight, a kindly land; one quite different from the nightmare world of "At the End of the Passage" or the cholera and plague-ridden death-house of "Without Benefit of Clergy". Because he understands, and indeed is part of, the setting, Kim is able to master it. In *Kim*, the power of India is reduced and restrained.

The influence of Twain on Kipling is again evident in *Kim*, for *Kim* and *Huckleberry Finn* (1884) have similar structures, characters and themes. Both picaresque novels concern a journey along a major artery in a quest for freedom by an older dependent man of a different race who is under the care and protection of an orphan boy. The boy's character is largely defined by his relation to and feelings about the man, and his rejection of traditional white ideas about other races. Both boys become increasingly committed to the older men who, in their kindliness and affection, become father figures. Both novels are seriously flawed at the end when the boys are persuaded by another white to forget their love, betray their admirable principles and assert their racial superiority just as the men are about to achieve their long-sought freedom. Huck's emotions are manipulated by Tom in the same way that Kim's are by Creighton. Then, quite suddenly in the final pages, the older men attain freedom and part from the boys whose lives must inevitably follow a different path.

The theme of *Kim* is the quest for identity by the white boy who is not a white boy, and Kim frequently asks the central questions of the novel: "Who is Kim?", "What am I?" The novel provides an answer

to these questions, focuses the various aspects of Kim's hybrid
personality, and resolves the conflict between heredity and environment
that is expressed in the opening lines of the eighth chapter:

> Something I owe to the soil that grew—
> More to the life that fed—
> But most to Allah Who gave me two
> Separate sides to my head.

Though Kim considers himself an Indian and is unaware of any
conflict until the chaplains explain his racial origins to him, the question
of his identity and allegiance is really settled before the novel begins.
Kim's most admirable and sympathetic qualities are his Indian ones and
we expect these to be dominant. But Kipling believes the collective
racial (English) identity is always more important than the personal
cultural (Indian) one, and the meaning of the novel is simply that blood
will tell: "Once a Sahib, always a Sahib."

Kim has a double personality and is torn by the antithetical demands
of the East and West. Though one usually remembers Kim as an
Eurasian; "though he was burned black as any native; though he spoke
the vernacular by preference, and his mother-tongue in a clipped,
uncertain sing-song; though he consorted on terms of perfect equality
with the small boys of the bazar; Kim was white"(5). His mother was
a nursemaid, his father an Irish soldier, and he was looked after by a
half-caste woman and educated on the streets of Lahore. He usually
thinks and dreams in Hindi; he prefers native food and eats like an
Indian; he sleeps curled up, native fashion; has an Oriental vagueness
about time, an Eastern resignation to fate and indifference to noise;
and he generally borrowed from all the customs of the country. But
he also has the white man's fear of snakes, a white cockiness and
aggressiveness, and a white respect for orders. During the crucial
encounter with the Russian and French spies, his white characteristics
become preponderant. He is roused by an Irish devil, thinks in English,
remembers he is white, takes a Sahib's point of view, gives orders
(which are obeyed) to his Indian superior Hurree Mookerjee, and when
the vital baggage is captured, distributes English kisses to the Woman of
Shamlegh. Kim's racial amalgamation is symbolized by the kit he
carries away from school: an English revolver, medicine-box and
compass, and an Indian robe, amulet and begging-gourd. His confusion
about his racial identity is indicated by his constant shift from the
vernacular to English and back again.

In the course of the novel, Kim, who is adept at disguises and pigmentation, dresses alternately as a Hindu, Moslem, Buddhist, Eurasian, and English civilian, soldier and schoolboy. His teachers are the Moslem Mahbub Ali, the Buddhist Teshoo Lama, the Hindu Hurree Mookerjee, and the Christian Creighton and Lurgan. He simultaneously assumes conflicting roles and follows conflicting paths. He plays the Great Game while he seeks the Way, and is at once Sahib and disciple, white and black, English and Indian. Well might the letter-writer ask him, as indeed he asks himself, "what manner of white boy art thou?"

Kim plays three principal roles in the novel: disciple, student and spy, and these roles are reflected in the tripartite structure of the book. The first section ends when Kim finds the red bull on the Mavericks' flag and is taken from the Lama by the chaplains. The second section concerns Kim's formal education — with the Regiment, at St. Xavier's and with Lurgan. In the final part Kim is reunited with the Lama and achieves his first professional success in the Great Imperial Spy Game. Kim is Indian in the first section, English (with Indian holidays) in the second, and English disguised as an Indian in the third. He is oblivious to English life in part one, rebellious in part two, and acquiescent and most obviously English in part three.

Kim's first role is disciple, his first teacher is the Lama. Kipling's choice of a Tibetan and a Buddhist to represent the spiritual aspects of India, whose nationality and religion the Lama does not possess, is a curious one.[39] As Kim remarks when he first sees the Lama, "he is no man of India". By using a Buddhist instead of a Moslem character, Kipling loads the plot, prepares us for Kim's desertion, and evades the problems of loyalty that would result if he involved Kim with an Indian. As a non-political foreigner, the Lama has no strong claim on Kim's fidelity, which is to the Moslems of Lahore, and the *chela* can leave the *guru* without feeling he has abandoned India.

Kipling's portrayal of the Lama is shallow and superficial. We are constantly told that he is deep in meditation, that he is illumining knowledge with brilliant insight, and considering vast matters, yet we never learn just what these meditations, illuminations and insights are. Instead of profound ideas, Kipling gives us capitalized Abstractions like Desire, Wheel, Way, Enlightenment, Search and Cause of Things. The Lama pronounces *"Om mane pudme hum,"* but if we want to know that it is a Tibetan invocation to Avalokitesvara, the omnipresent universal spirit or divine essence of Buddha, we must find out for ourselves. Though Kipling is tolerant of Buddhism, he has only the most elementary and general understanding of it. We need only

compare the Lama with Forster's Professor Godbole to realize at
once that Forster commands a knowledge of Hinduism and can present
a living and believable philosophical Hindu character, and that this
is quite beyond Kipling's powers. Kipling calls the Lama a child and
Kim says he is quite mad, and it is this vague, childish and affectionate
aspect of his character that prevails in the novel. Kipling's attitude is
one of tolerant pity that comes from a sense of inborn superiority.

The relationship of the orphan *chela* to the celibate *guru* is filial,
and a second quest in this novel of many quests is that of a father for
a son and a son for a father. As the Lama admits, "My *chela* is to me as
is a son to the unenlightened"(273). "Thou leanest on me in the body,
Holy One," says Kim, "but I lean on thee for some other things"
(272), parental affection and emotional security. Just as the Lama's
heart went out to Kim, so Kim's heart is drawn to the Lama.

Their relationship is purely familial and emotional, for despite his
extensive discipleship with the Lama, Kim learns nothing from his
teacher. What the Lama calls Illusion is for Kim the only Reality. It
is not, as Kim suggests, that the Lama's lesson is too profound, but
that it is, according to Kipling, *racially* impossible for Kim to understand the Lama. His whole way of life is refuted by Kim who rejects
Nirvana and follows the Great Game instead.

Though he has committed himself to the Great Game, Kim's
conflicts and self-questioning continue to the very end of the novel
when heredity triumphs over environment and color conquers culture.
When Kim wakes from his deep convalescent sleep, he wants to get
into the world again and ponders his identity for at least the fourth
time in the book. Before he hears the Lama's religious revelation,
he firmly roots himself in the reality of daily existence. "Roads were
meant to be walked upon, houses to be lived in, cattle to be driven,
fields to be tilled, and men and women to be talked to. They were all
real and true — solidly planted upon the feet — perfectly comprehensible
— clay of his clay, neither more nor less" (282). When the excited
Lama tells him he has finally attained Nirvana and offers his faithful,
albeit obtuse, *chela* Salvation — "the wise Soul loosed itself from the
silly Body and went free" — Kim grasps only the material aspect and
responds, "A marvel indeed. Two days and two nights without food!"
As the Lama ecstatically describes his withdrawal from the Great
Soul, and the reunification of his Body and Spirit, Kim has filial
concern and placidly asks, "Wast thou very wet?" (Here Kipling gives
us comedy when he is trying to be serious.) When the Lama offers
Salvation and freedom from the Wheel of Things, Kim prefers to mesh

his soul with the reality of the world and become a cog-wheel connected with the machinery of the Game. It is entirely appropriate that when he enters the service he completely loses the personal identity he had desperately wanted to establish and, like E.23, enjoys the dignity of a letter and a number. Perhaps this is inevitable in Kipling's works, for even the wild and wonderful Mowgli is domesticated by the English and becomes an employee of the Forest Service.

Ironically enough, Kim's master is instrumental in alienating him from the Way, and leading him to his second role as student. In a central passage, and one characteristic of Kipling in that it is at cross-purposes with his intended effect, Kim says:

> "I was made wise by thee, Holy One," forgetting the little play just ended [Kim as healer]; forgetting St. Xavier's; forgetting his white blood; forgetting even the Great Game as he stooped, Mohammedan fashion, to touch his master's feet in the dust of the Jain temple. "My teaching I owe to thee. I have eaten thy bread three years. My time is finished. I am loosed from the schools. I come to thee!". . .[Lama:] "I did well—I did well when I gave thee up to the armed men on that black night"(190).

Kim has been made wise not by the teaching of the Lama, but by the money that the Lama has paid for Kim's tuition at a parochial public school, which has provided a training for action, not for meditation[40]. When the Lama instructs Kim to abstain from action, Kim replies this is unbefitting a Sahib. It is precisely the influences that Kipling protests Kim is "forgetting" that are the ones which define his identity: his white blood and his white school, "for St. Xavier's looks down on boys who 'go native altogether'.[41] One must never forget that one is a Sahib, and that some day, when examinations are passed, one will command natives"(126). Kim's other influences— Buddhist, Moslem and Hindu-Jain— are mentioned in this passage, but they are minor ones. For even as Kim speaks he is involving the unwitting and unwilling Lama in the Great Game by taking him away from his search for the river on the Plains and into the Hills for counter-espionage work.

It is equally ironic that Kim should willingly submit to school and be transformed into a Sahib, for he had spent his whole life avoiding school and discipline. Kim is unhappy at school, uncomfortable in tight clothes, lonely among white men; he tries to run away and is joyful when he can escape during vacations. The values and regimentation of school and white life are totally alien to everything he stands for and everything that is likeable and admirable in his curious, daring picaresque and rootless character. But his collision with the white values of the school is balanced by his ability to learn the white lessons, and he soon adjusts. After three years, the "Sahib-ization" is so complete that Kim must be given six months leave to become "de-Englishised," so that he will once more be fit for the spy service, his third and final role.

The white characters in *Kim* are all partially "de-Englishised," and they share Hurree's ethnological interest in the Indians, for professional if not for intellectual reasons. Like the Strickland of the earlier stories, who appears briefly at the Delhi railroad station to help E.23 escape, Creighton and Lurgan "held the extraordinary theory that a Police-man [or spy] in India should try to know as much about the natives as the natives themselves".[42]

It is precisely Strickland's knowledge of the natives, Lurgan's linguistic talents and Creighton's ability to plumb the Oriental mind which, combined in Kim, make him such a rare and perfect player of the Great Game. Though agent E.23 expounds the dangers of being a spy, he himself escapes misfortune by a simple ruse, and Kim never seems to be aware of any risk or in any danger, especially when fighting Russians (i.e. Asians). When Hurree commands the Russian spies to stop shooting at Kim, they obey him and allow their important papers and equipment to be captured. "This collapse of their Great Game . . . this panicky bolt into the night, had come about through no craft of Hurree's or contrivance of Kim's, but simply, beautifully, and inevitably as the capture of Mahbub's *faquir*-friends by the zealous young policeman at Umballa"(248).

Though Kipling's attitude toward war and diplomacy in *Kim* is extremely naive and the Russian spies are treated as stereotyped and simple-minded villains, Anglo-Russian rivalry in India was intense in Kipling's time and Russia was a very real enemy.[43] In 1846, two thousand miles had separated the English and Russian frontiers. Thirty years later, they were only five hundred miles apart, with only the unstable power of the Amir of Kabul between them. In 1884 the Russians occupied Merv in northwest Afghanistan which caused great alarm in both England and India, and the Afghan-Indian and Afghan-Russian borders were not settled until 1893 and 1895 respectively. This uneasiness about and hostility toward Russia is reflected in Kipling's strongly anti-Russian story of an English officer imprisoned in Siberia, "The Man Who Was" (*Life's Handicap*), as well as in Dan's ambition in "The Man Who Would Be King" to provide an army ready to attack Russia when she tries for India. But Kim's reasons for becoming a spy have nothing to do with the Russian threat and are trivial and superficial. His desire to be a spy comes from his boyish delight in the Game, his urge for excitement and power, and his pride in departmental praise. He finds it fun to kick the Russian in the groin, and he hopes that some day he might be almost as great as Mahbub Ali.

The reason that Kim, and ultimately the novel itself, are so disappointing is that Kim so naively agrees to be manipulated by Creighton and turned into a spy against and betrayer of the very people and country that nurtured him. Like many other Kipling characters, Kim's identity is established by and through his work, and the one vocation that Kim is especially suited for is espionage. If being white means being a spy, then Kim's moral identity is lost when his racial identity is found. The moral compromise involved in becoming a spy is never once raised in the novel, and what ought to be the central problem is carefully avoided. Even the Holy Lama, who is defined in the novel by his goodness and morality, never tells Kim that spying is wrong – he even encourages it. Kim sees himself only as a spy against the Russians and does not realize he will soon be forced to undermine the India he once loved by spying against his former friends. Compared to the tortured and confused spy Razumov in *Under Western Eyes*, Kim's self-righteousness and lack of moral awareness seem very superficial. Thus Kim joins the ranks of Mahbub and Hurree who have sold themselves to the English. Kipling creates a marvellous character in the first section of the novel, but unintentionally makes him morally reprehensible in the following section.

Despite these serious limitations, Kim is unique among Kipling characters in his ability to understand, appreciate and control both the English and the Indian worlds. He fits equally well into both worlds but does not truly belong to either. Though he lacks self-awareness and blindly accepts his role as spy, he discovers his racial identity. Though he is victimized by the colonial system and made into a Sahib for purposes of espionage, he is nevertheless deeply involved with the Indians and sympathetic to their viewpoint. He does achieve a meaningful emotional, if not intellectual, relationship with the Lama, Mahbub and Hurree. He is, according to the Lama who emphasizes his Indian qualities, "Temperate, kindly, wise, of ungrudging disposition a merry heart upon the road, never forgetting, learned, truthful, courteous" (282-3). Yet he is also, like the men of the earlier stories, disciplined, resourceful, capable, responsible and courageous.

2

E. M. FORSTER:
A PASSAGE TO INDIA

1. *Forster and Kipling*

KIPLING was the first major English writer to deal extensively and seriously with the British colonies, and he virtually invented the genre of colonial fiction. An immensely productive author, he had already published seven volumes of stories and poems when he sailed for England at the age of 24 in 1889, and like the young Goethe and Byron, became famous overnight. He soon became the most popular and influential author of the age, and during his lifetime more than fifteen million copies of his books were sold in England and America. Thus, Kipling's idea of India and the Indians was the one that overwhelmingly prevailed until 1924, when *A Passage to India* was published, and well beyond. According to Thornton, "the imperial principle, animating an imperial code, remained the dynamic in the thought and action of the governing classes of England until *after* the close of the twentieth century's second world war".[1]

But when Forster visited India in 1912–13 and again in 1921–22, he found that his own experience was quite unlike Kipling's, and that from his point of view, Kipling's ideas about India were quite unsatisfactory. One of the intentions of *A Passage to India* is to refute and correct Kipling's views about the country and people that were generally held by most Englishmen of his time, and Forster specifically confronts and opposes Kipling's ideas throughout the novel.

Forster's India is no longer the romantic and adventurous land of daring warfare and imperial conquest glorified by Kipling, though the power and threat of India remain fearsome. Forster opposed Kipling's patriotic jingoism with restraint and sensitivity, and satirized the national anthem and public school, the Empire and White Man's Burden. D.H. Lawrence was probably thinking of these very concepts, which Kipling took seriously, when he wrote, "*A Passage to India* interested me very much. At least the repudiation of our white bunk is genuine, sincere, and pretty thorough, it seems to me."[2]

Forster and his hero Fielding value individualism, personal relations, tolerance and understanding, and these Bloomsbury values are opposed to Kipling's literary and political ideas. Whereas Forster emphasizes the moral and intellectual aspects of human experience, Kipling stresses the physical. In Kipling's story "Thrown Away", the pathetic young hero was sensitive and took things seriously, and these qualities cause his suicide. The English officials portrayed by both writers share the *same* values, but appear in entirely different lights, for Kipling's heroes become Forster's villains. The military officers, whom Kipling respects and praises, are the most vile and hateful of Forster's characters. Major Callendar, Aziz's superior, deliberately subjects Nureddin, his Indian patient, to physical cruelties, and boasts about it afterwards. The Army subaltern is a bully and a boor who calls Fielding a "swine" when he alone courageously defends Aziz.

Forster's openness and flexibility of mind, his sense of relativity in culture and ethics, his sympathy and respect for other nationalities and civilizations, are in direct contrast to Kipling's rigid ethnocentric nationalism. In *A Passage to India,* Forster belittles the pretence of European moral and cultural superiority and denies the English claim to the title of civilization. Kipling emphasizes the gulf between the races, and in stories like "Without Benefit of Clergy" illustrates the disasters suffered by those who try to bridge this gulf. Forster believes in the possibility of one world merging with the other; for him, a passage to India is a movement toward the friendship that Fielding and Aziz develop. Aziz tells Mrs Moore she is Oriental, and Fielding also understands and appreciates Indian culture. He is easternized as Aziz is westernized, and their personalities and cultures complement one another. The English Club is the focus of cultural ethnocentrism, and as Leonard Woolf, once a white sahib in Ceylon, writes, it is the "symbol and centre of British imperialism. . . . It had normally a curious air of slight depression, but at the same time exclusiveness, superiority, isolation. . . . The atmosphere was terribly masculine and public school."[3] Forster would have us reject the bitter tradition of mistrust that is engendered there.

The difference between Kipling and Forster's attitude toward English-Indian social relations is revealed in their respective bridge parties, which attempt to bridge the gulf between the East and West. Kipling stresses the great gulfs of miscomprehension, feels that any real understanding is impossible, and mocks such attempts at friendship when Wali Dad, a westernized Moslem, ironically speaks of "the Commissioner's tennis parties where the English stand on one side and the natives on the other, in order to promote social intercourse throughout the Empire."[4] Forster's Turton, the Collector (of Revenue) or District Officer, who speaks with twenty-five years experience, sums up Kipling's views on this subject: "I have never known anything but disaster result when English people and Indians attempt to be intimate socially."[5] The failure of his party is inevitable, for as the Indian ambassador K.M. Panikkar writes, "As a result of this doctrine of prestige and race superiority the Europeans in India, however long they lived there, remained strangers in the country. An unbridgeable chasm existed between them and the people, which was still true till the very end of British rule in India."[6]

Forster also disagrees with Kipling's optimistic Victorian assumptions that progress is clearly taking place, and that law and order are dutifully being maintained, when the latter solemnly writes of Malaya (in a sentence that could easily be mistaken for Forster's ironic style), "Into this land God put first gold and tin, and after these the Englishman who floats companies, obtains concessions and goes forward."[7] On the contrary, Forster is extremely sceptical about the idea of progress, and writes in his central credo, "What I Believe" (1939), "the nations of today behave to each other worse than they ever did in the past, they cheat, rob, bully and bluff, make war without notice, and kill as many women and children as possible; whereas primitive tribes were at all events restrained by taboos".[8]

The first, and perhaps the most important of Kipling's values that Forster specifically attacks in *A Passage to India*, are those of the English public school. Whereas Kipling worshipped his school and celebrated it in *Stalkey & Co.* (1899), Forster was intensely unhappy at school and loathed it. Most of the Indian Civil Service men came from the public schools, so that the public school code of duty and self-sacrifice became the guiding principle of the imperial administration. Kipling's version of this code is expressed most idealistically in "On the City Wall", where he writes that men in the ICS "die, or kill themselves by overwork, or are worried to death or broken in health and hope in order that the land may be protected from death and sickness, famine and war."[9] In stories like "At the End of the Passage", "The Last Relief" and "William the Conqueror", Kipling gave this code a literary form, and he became identified in the popular imagination with the public school traditions.

Kipling often draws analogies between school and military life, and was fond of using the public school metaphor. In "The Last

Relief", Hamerton's speech to Haydon concluding "I'm afraid—I'm very much afraid—that you will have to go down" to duty,[10] has the reluctant yet forceful tone of a Headmaster asking a prefect to perform an unpleasant task for the sake of the school. The central concept here is discipline and the submission of all varieties of personality to the group, the school, the regiment, and the Colonial Service, all of which must stand united. Kipling's world allows no variation, no flexibility; he emphasizes the law of the pack, and sees the individual as a dispensable part of the total group. When men die during an epidemic in "The Last Relief", Kipling writes "The chain of men parted for an instant at the stroke [of death], but it closed up again, and continued to drag the empire forward, and not one living link of it rang false or was weak."[11]

Forster, on the other hand, is anti-authoritarian and opposes this militaristic attitude, which he expresses in Kipling's language. Aziz speaks regretfully of the English closing their broken ranks against the Indians; and after Aziz is arrested, McBryde tells Fielding "at a time like this there's no room for—well—personal views. The man who doesn't toe the line is lost . . . . If you leave the line, you leave a gap in the line" (171). Fielding rejects this view and he alone opposes the entire English community in his declaration of Aziz's innocence. This refusal to be a link in the chain, a cog in the machinery or to follow the herd instinct is a tribute to Fielding's individuality and his loyalty to Aziz.

Fielding's antithesis is Ronny Heaslop, one of the typical products of the public school, who believes the English are in India only to do their work and carry out their duty, and have no time to be pleasant. Ronny's lack of human feeling upsets Mrs Moore and reminds her of his public-schooldays. Her answer to Ronny is one of religious love that stresses the essential fellowship and unity of all men. Mrs Moore's religious attitude is entirely different from that of her son, who "approved of religion as long as it endorsed the National Anthem, but objected when it attempted to influence his life . . . . Ronny's religion was of the sterilized Public School brand, which never goes bad, even in the tropics. Wherever he entered, mosque, cave, or temple, he retained the spiritual outlook of the Fifth Form" (52, 257). It is precisely on these grounds that Forster criticizes Kipling's *Letters of Travel,* his only extensive statement about Kipling. Forster emphasizes his

arrested development; the young gentleman was as clever as

ever, but he failed to grow up. . . he retained the mentality of a
Boy Scout. . . the real tragedy is that here is a writer of great
genius whose equipment has never developed. Few men have
seen as much as Kipling; few men have experienced so little in
the true sense of experience. . . he inspects civilisation as it were
from the window of the Fifth Form room.[12]

In opposition to Kipling, Forster shows how inadequately the public
schools train men for India. Ronny insists that experience, in Forster's
sense of trial or experiment, would not help Adela understand India
"because she could not interpret it. A Public School, London
University [not Cambridge, like Hamidullah and presumably Fielding],
a year at a crammer's, a particular sequence of posts in a particular
province, a fall from a horse and a touch of fever were presented to her
as the only training by which Indians and all who reside in their country
can be understood" (81). Kipling's masculine and wonderfully efficient
woman worker William in "William the Conqueror" had just this sort
of experience, and Kipling finds it quite satisfactory. During the four
years she spent with her brother Scott in the ICS, "Twice she had
been nearly drowned while fording a river on *horseback;* once she had
been run away with on a camel. . . and had wound up her experiences
by six weeks of typhoid *fever.*"[13] When a suitor tried to talk to her
about Wordsworth's "Excursion," William explained that poetry made
her head ache. Forster exposes this English philistinism and proud
ignorance of the arts, and suggests that people who deny their own
culture are unlikely to appreciate a different one.

Forster also attacks Kipling's racial and political ideas, both of
which are related to his public school attitudes. Like most other
imperialists, Kipling believes in the theory of the martial and non-
martial Indian races. He respects the former as fierce warriors whom
the British recruit for their mercenary Army, and tends to scorn the
others, particularly the well-educated and westernized *babus.* In
"Letters of Marque" Kipling condescendingly praises the warrior
tribes:

> The Rahtor, who comes of fighting stock, is a fine animal, and
> well-bred; the Hara, who seems to be more compactly built, is
> also a fine animal; but for a race that show blood in every line
> of their frame. . . the financial class of Rajputana appears to be
> the most remarkable.[14]

A similar speech is made by the loathsome subaltern at the Club meeting right after Aziz's arrest.

> Give me the sporting type of native, give me the Gurkhas, give
> me Rajputs, give me Jats, give me the Punjabi, give me Sikhs,
> give me Marathas, Bhils, Afridis and Pathans, and really if it
> comes to that, I don't mind if you give me the scums of the
> bazaars. Properly led, mind. I'd lead them anywhere—. (184)

Ronny also subscribes to this theory, and at the Bridge Party explains
to his visitors, with Mrs Turton's approval, that educated Indians are
craven and seditious at heart, and only the Pathan is manly and loyal.
According to Ronny the cowardly "squealing" Indians are the *babus*
who, like Grish Chunder Dé, M.A., in Kipling's "The Head of the
District", run from their duties during a crisis. But Forster deliberately
praises the *babus* at one point in the novel, and treats the Nawab's
Eurasian driver sympathetically, while Eurasians are invariably objects
of Kipling's scorn.

The other racial theoretician and student of Oriental Pathology is
the Superintendent of Police, McBryde, who believes that all unfortunate
natives born in the tropics are criminals at heart.[15] McBryde was born
in Karachi and seems to contradict his own theory until, after attacking
Aziz's sexual morality with a chaster-than-thou attitude, he is caught
in flagrante delicto committing adultery with Miss Derek.

During Aziz's trial, McBryde remarks as a general truth and scientific
fact that Indians are physically attracted by the English, but not *vice
versa*. McBryde's "truth" is contrary to the facts, for Aziz is revolted
by Adela's angular body, tiny breasts and freckles, while she finds
him handsome and admires his physical beauty, thick hair and fine
skin ("the lady is so uglier than the gentleman"). This was an explosive
issue in 1924. In Kipling's stories, as we have seen, Indian women
and English men have disastrous liaisons, but English women are
never attracted to Indian men, let alone rejected by them.

Kipling usually treats Indians as an undifferentiated mass, as character
types (not individuals), or in a completely negative light. In "The Man
Who Would be King", the "kings" fire into their own men as well
as into the enemy. In his most characteristic stories of Indian
life, he deals with prostitution and corruption in "On the City
Wall", deception and murder in "In the House of Suddhoo", jealousy
and vengeance in "Dray Wara Yow Dee", and mutilation and cruelty
in "Beyond the Pale".

For Forster, life is a matter of individual lives. The convincing and authentic second chapter, an Indian social scene where Aziz and his friends discuss the possibilities of friendship with the English, is a welcome innovation in colonial fiction. Forster expertly portrays the Indians speaking to each other in the vernacular and to the British in colloquial Indianized English, for he had intimately observed Indian social life while private secretary to the Maharajah of Dewas Senior. The juxtaposition of Indian and English social scenes, like the contrast of Indian and English physical types, shows the attractive warm vitality of the former and the unpleasant cold sterility of the latter. Fielding, who observes the civilized gestures of well-bred Indians, contrasts them to the boorish manners of the English.

The third area in which Forster specifically opposes Kipling is in politics. Kipling's anti-democratic views and distrust of Parliament are most notoriously exhibited in "The Enlightenment of Pagett, M.P.," and in the foolish Member for Lower Tooting who needlessly intrudes in "Without Benefit of Clergy". Turton speaks disdainfully of the cranks and cravens in the British Parliament, and Ronny insists his principles are quite distinct from those of a Labour Member or a sentimental literary man.

During the crisis before Aziz's trial, two references are made to important events in nineteenth-century Indian history, the Mutiny and the Ilbert Bill. In Kipling's *Kim*, Kim and the Lama encounter an old native officer who remained loyal to the British during the 1857 Mutiny and who recounts his exploits for their benefit. Though he admits, "I am an outcast among my own kin, and my cousin's blood is wet on my sabre," he is proud of his loyalty to the English. The old officer mentions the *Indian* brutality with extreme horror: he has "seen the land from Delhi south awash with blood. . .[the Indians] chose to kill the Sahibs' wives and children."[16] In contrast to these sentiments, Aziz proudly tells Fielding that his grandfather fought the British in the Mutiny and he would do the same. And McBryde alludes to the Indian brutality when he tells Fielding that the Mutiny records should be his Bible in India, conveniently forgetting the well-authenticated *English* brutality during that uprising.[17]

The second historical allusion is to the controversy in 1883 over the Ilbert Bill, which would have allowed Indian magistrates to try Europeans. When McBryde tells Adela that she will have to testify and be cross-examined before an Indian magistrate, he grew very bitter over these "fruits of democracy" and longed for the autocracy of the past. Turton also longed for the good old days when an Englishman could do exactly as he pleased, with no questions asked.

Both McBryde and Turton are reactionaries who regret the English concessions to justice enacted by the Ilbert Bill and similar progressive legislation.

Kipling worked on the semi-official Allahabad *Pioneer* from 1887 to 1889 and supported its opposition to the Ilbert Bill and to all Indian political aspirations. When Aziz ironically quotes the old charges of Indian brutality, "We will rob every man and rape every woman from Peshawar to Calcutta," he claims that the English will quote it every week in the *Pioneer* as propaganda. Thus, a great number of Kipling's social and political ideas are completely opposed and reversed in *A Passage to India*, and when spoken by the English, are neatly exposed and undercut by Forster's irony.

2.   *Background and Politics*

When asked about the composition of *A Passage to India*, which he wrote over a period of twelve years, Forster told the *Paris Review* interviewers, "I had a great deal of difficulty with the novel, and thought I would never finish it. I began it in 1912, and then came the war. I took it with me when I returned to India in 1921, but found what I had written wasn't India at all. It was like sticking a photograph on a picture. However, I couldn't *write* it when I was in India. When I got away, I could get on with it."[18] Rose Macaulay is therefore inaccurate when she writes that the novel "deals with the India of one period [1912], is written largely from material collected and from a point of view derived *from that* [1912] *period*, and was published twelve years later."[19] Actually, Forster writes about India from a *1924*, not a 1912, viewpoint. He depicts the reactionary pre-World War I colonial ideas and attitudes of 1912 (when the book takes place) as if they still existed in 1922-24 (the dates of composition and publication). He therefore intends the people in the novel to seem totally unaware of the vast changes that had occurred in India and the rest of the world since 1912. The dramatic tension between the pre-war point of view of the characters and the post-war point of view of the author, intensifies the political significance of the novel and heightens its persuasive power and irony.

The important post-war-political events have been ignored by critics like Gransden who mistakenly write, "the wartime gap would *not* have had much significance, for the World War had *little* effect on India, where the social and political pattern imposed by the British continued largely *unchanged* until almost the time of the final withdrawal".[20] Even Trilling states, "its data were gathered in 1912 and 1922, *before* the full spate of Indian nationalism".[21] On the contrary, the 1912-22 period was of the greatest significance for India and had a profound effect on the country, and it is precisely during this period that the forces of Indian nationalism first began to operate with potent effect.

One small example will suggest the difference between the two periods. As the "Bridge party" commences, Mrs Turton haughtily instructs Mrs Moore and Adela, "You're superior to everyone in India except one or two of the Ranis, and they're on an equality." In "Reflections on India" (1922), Forster writes, "the lady who said to me eight years ago, 'Never forget that you're superior to every native in India except the Rajas and they're on an equality', is now a silent, if not extinct species. But she had lived her life, and she has done her work."[22]

An understanding of the overwhelmingly important events that occurred in India and in the entire world between 1917 and 1922 places *A Passage to India* in historical perspective, and emphasizes the political significance and political implications of race relations, fear of riots, English justice and government, Hindu-Moslem unity, Indian Native States, nationalism and the independence movement in the novel. Forster himself says, "You cannot understand the modern Indians unless you realise that politics occupy them passionately and constantly."[23]

Between Forster's first and second visits to India in 1912 and 1921, the world experienced the Great War, Wilson's Fourteen Points (1918) and the League of Nations (1919), the Russian Revolution, and the revolutionary Sinn Fein movement (1918-1921) that led to the creation of the Irish Free State.[24] World War I, like the other events, provided a violent stimulus for Indian nationalism, for "agitation against the British. . . did not reach formidable proportions until the twentieth century, and particularly after World War I".[25] The fifth of Wilson's Fourteen Points demanded "A free, open-minded and absolutely impartial adjustment of all colonial claims," and seriously weakened the imperialist position. In Asia the idea of the self-determination of peoples was acclaimed as a doctrine of liberation. In 1917, Lenin published the inflammatory *Imperialism: The Highest State of Capitalism,* and imperialism meant something totally different

after Lenin's insistence on the liberation of subject peoples. In 1921,
for example, Grigory Zinoviev, Chairman of the Comintern and
Politburo member, told the predominantly Moslem Congress of the
Peoples of the East in Baku, Georgia: "The Communist International
turns today to the people of the East and says to them, 'Brothers,
we summon you to a Holy War [the Moslem *jihad* against the infidel],
first of all against British imperialism."[26]

Immediately after the War, India experienced Gandhi's rise to
prominence, the Montagu Declaration (1917) and the First Government
of India Act (1919), the Amritsar Massacre (1919), the Moplah
Rebellion (1921), and the Khalifat Movements (1921-22). Gandhi
returned from his career as a lawyer and political agitator in South
Africa in 1914. In 1919 he launched his first campaign of passive
resistance against the Rowlatt Acts that permitted judges to try
political cases without juries and extended the power of internment
without trial to provincial governments. Gandhi initiated civil dis-
obedience in 1920, and was arrested and sentenced to prison in 1922.
The first important concession to Indian nationalism was made in the
Montagu Declaration which provided for the gradual development of
self-governing institutions that would eventually lead to Dominion
status. This proposal was embodied in the First Government of India
Act which opened the road to parliamentary government, and was
the first serious challenge to British rule since the 1857 Mutiny.

The most notorious and violent post-war event was the Amritsar
Massacre. Without warning, the English General Dyer broke up a
prohibited meeting of ten thousand people by firing 1650 rounds,
killing over three hundred people and wounding over a thousand more.
He stopped only when his ammunition was exhausted. Snyder writes
that

> Among the orders passed by General Dyer at Amritsar was an
> order that has been styled 'Crawling Order' . . . The order was to
> the effect that no Indians should be allowed to pass through the
> street, but if they wanted to pass they must go on all fours
> and pickets were placed at certain points in the street to enforce
> obedience to this order . . . Within a few minutes after he
> had passed the order and put the pickets, twelve persons
> had to be arrested for being insolent and he ordered them
> to be taken into custody, and the police took them through
> the street and the picket enforced the crawling order on
> them.[27]

There is an oblique but unmistakable reference to this infamous crawling order in *A Passage to India*. At the height of the ugly British hatred, hysteria and fear, when the innocent Aziz is freed and the mob is rioting, just after Major Callendar boasts of his medical cruelties to the "buck nigger" Nureddin and says "there's not such a thing as cruelty after a thing like this," Mrs Turton virulently responds:

> Exactly, and remember it afterwards, you men. You're weak, weak, weak. Why, they ought to *crawl* from here to the caves on their hands and knees whenever an Englishwoman's in sight, they oughtn't to be spoken to, they ought to be spat at, they ought to be ground into the dust (216). (Italics mine.)

The bitter epilogue is that though General Dyer was retired after the Massacre, the readers of the London *Morning Post* rallied to his support and subscribed a testimonial of £26,000.

The Moplah Rebellion took place on the *Malabar* Coast in August 1921, two years after Amritsar. Several thousand fanatical Moslems were killed by troops and violent crowds after they had skinned alive and slaughtered thousands of Hindus. The Marabar caves would remind every one who knew India of the recent horrors on the Malabar Coast.

The Khalifat was the only mass movement in the recent political history of India in which the Hindus and Moslems collaborated fully. The Indians demanded that the Sultan of Turkey and caliph of all Islam, who had recently been defeated in the Great War, should not be deposed or deprived of his power in the Arabian peninsula. (T.E. Lawrence had successfully led the Arab Revolt against the Sultan and had promised his followers independence.) In 1922, while in India, Forster wrote a sympathetic article on the Khalifat movement in which he said, the Indian Moslem "believes that under God's will the guardianship of Holy Places has passed to the Turks, and that Constantinople itself has become half-holy. . . [this belief] is decent, it is human, and even if it cannot be furthered it should not be wantonly insulted."[28]

Finally, Forster enlarged his own experience and ideas about colonialism by working with the International Red Cross in Alexandria from November 1915 until January 1919. In 1921 he was commissioned by the Labour Party Research Department to write on British colonial policy in Egypt. In his pamphlet, *The Government of Egypt*, he describes England's broken pledges and mistreatment of Egypt, and recommends independence. He criticizes the British High Commissioner,

Lord Cromer, for his profound distrust of Orientals, and asserts Cromer's sympathy with Nationalism was purely academic. Forster's social and political attitudes in this work anticipate *A Passage to India*, for he writes that "I have walked alone, both in the native quarters of the towns and in the country, and have always met courtesy and kindness," and that Cromer's colonial administrators and "still more their women-folk, introduce a racial arrogance from which the regular Anglo-Egyptian officials are free."[29]

The political themes of *A Passage to India* are crucial to the meaning of the novel, and are closely related to the social and philosophical ideas. Forster says that "the political side of it was an aspect I wanted to express,"[30] and his political purpose was to ameliorate the world in a small way by helping Indian aspirations. The novel was a set book for the Indian Civil Service, and Forster claims "It had some political influence—it caused people to think of the link between India and Britain and to doubt if that link was altogether of a healthy nature."[31] As the Indian writer Nirad Chaudhuri states, it "became a powerful weapon in the hands of the anti-imperialists, and was made to contribute its share to the disappearance of British rule in India".[32]

Forster's political reasoning is inductive; he begins with individuals and then moves to nations. The enormous difficulties that Aziz encounters when he prepares the expedition to the caves, suggests in miniature the difficulties of social life in all of India, and the multifarious differences that separate races and religions. Forster believes that colonial problems are primarily the result of personal misunderstanding and mutual incomprehension. He believes the personal relationship is most important to the Oriental, and that in the East, the individual must succeed as an individual or he has failed.

The opening description of Chandrapore emphasizes the physical opposition of the Indians in the squalid city near the river and the English in the civil station on the hill. In the next chapter, Aziz and his friends immediately introduce the social-political theme with which the novel is largely concerned: whether friendship with an Englishman is possible, and the contrapuntal chapters of the "Mosque" section reflect upon this question. The pleasant meeting in the mosque is followed by the frigidity of the Club; the Indians discuss the "Bridge Party" invitation, and the party fails. This disastrous party, Ronny's boorish and rude interruption of Fielding's tea party, the failure of the Bhattacharyas to fulfil their invitation, and the Nawab Bahadur's car accident, all indicate that friendship between a dominant and subservient people is rarely possible. The final answer to the question of friendship is emphatically negative: English and Indians cannot be friends until Indians are politically independent. Aziz's vow to Fielding, "India shall be a nation! . . . We may hate one another but we hate you most . . . we shall drive every blasted Englishman into the sea, and then . . . you and I shall be friends"(322), echoes the belief of the Hindu nationalist Bankim Chatterjee: "So long as the conqueror-conquered relationship will last between English and Indians, and so long as even in our present degraded condition we shall remember our former national glory, there cannot be any hope of lessening the racial hatred."[33] *A Passage to India* embodies the truth that Orientals hate their European oppressors.

Forster's answer to such political hatred, which he again presents on the individual level, is an ideal of personal behaviour and personal relations that is perhaps the major theme of the book, for it is echoed by three sympathetic characters, English and Indian, and embodied in the actions and fundamental good will of the hero, Fielding. Mrs. Moore expresses the beliefs of Aziz and Hamidullah when she appeals to her uncharitable son with a plea for "Good will and more good will and more good will" (52), and begins to quote I. Corinthians xiii.1, " 'Though I speak with the tongues of . . .' men and of angels, and have not charity, I am become as sounding brass, or a tinkling cymbal." Forster also emphasizes the need for kindness in "Reflections on India" and writes that

> The decent Anglo-Indian of today realizes that the great blunder of the past is neither political nor economic nor educational, but social. . . The mischief has been done, and though friendship between individuals will continue and courtesies between high officials increase, there is little hope now of spontaneous intercourse between two races . . . Never in history did ill-breeding contribute so much towards the dissolution of an Empire.[34]

The potent justification of the truth of Forster's social and political beliefs, which are fundamentally religious (though he is opposed to institutionalized and sectarian Christianity), comes from the Indians themselves. Forster's insistence on the need for kindness, charity and good will and his emphasis on the disastrous political effects of ill-breeding, are at the core of the charge made against the British by Gandhi: that they "were 'incompetent' to deal with the problems of India—which were not primarily administrative at all, but *social and religious*".[35] And Vinoba Bhave, a contemporary Indian saint and

Gandhi's adopted son, criticizes the West in purely Forsterian terms: "You have developed the head; the heart did not keep pace. With us it was the opposite—it was with the development of the heart that we have been concerned in India."[36] Adela's sacrifice was rightly rejected by the Indians because it did not include her heart.

In *A Passage to India* Forster also attacks the traditional (and mythical) justification of imperialism, that the natives are better off under English domination. Sir Alan Burns, former Governor-General of the Gold Coast, presents this argument as late as 1957: "the subject peoples of the British Empire have greater liberty and better conditions of living than many of the inhabitants of independent countries".[37] Fielding deliberately rejects this view, and in a political discussion with Indians is too honest to give the conventional answer that England holds India for her benefit, which Ronny gives earlier in the novel. Aziz's assertion that there can be no self-respect without independence expresses Forster's understanding that Indians yearn for political freedom and do not care about economics, that they prefer to be ruled badly by themselves than well by others, and that no amount of progress can compensate for lack of liberty and personal dignity, a lack that degrades every aspect of personal, cultural, social and moral life. This belief has always been held by Indian nationalists. Deshbandu Das, in his presidential address to the Indian National Congress in the 1920s said, "Morally, we are becoming a nation of slaves....Intellectually we have become willing victims to the imposition of a foreign culture upon us . . . there is inherent in subjection something which injures national life and hampers its growth and fulfillment."[38]

The trial of Aziz is a political allegory on this theme. Adela's accusation of Aziz is also Britain's accusation of India— that she is poor, backward, dirty, disorganized, uncivilized, promiscuous, uncontrollable, violent—in short, that she needs imperialism.[39] His innocence is equivalent to India's right to freedom, which is symbolized by Aziz's transformation from subservient and passive before the trial to independent and nationalistic after it. Before his arrest he is not interested in kicking the British out of India; after his release he is more formidable and proudly announces that he has become anti-British.[40]

Adela's echo also has political implications, for it functions as a sonant conscience, sounding doubts about her charge against Aziz and expressing the guilt and fear of the English imperialists. When Mrs Moore remains secluded, and Ronny supports Adela's charges, "the echo flourished, raging up and down like a nerve in the faculty of her hearing, and the noise in the cave, so unimportant intellectually, was prolonged over the surface of her life" (194). It resounds and haunts her periodically when she considers her accusation, diminishes when she thinks of retracting the false charges, and disappears only when she tears the veil of illusion and releases Aziz. After the trial when she tells Fielding she no longer has any secrets, the evil echo leaves her and discharges itself into the Indian atmosphere of hatred, hostility, recrimination and animosity.

Finally, Forster's political ideas are prophetic. Aziz predicts not only the Hindu-Moslem unity against the British, but also that independence will be achieved in the next European war. And he prophesies a conference of Oriental statesmen which takes place thirty years later (1955) in Bandung, Indonesia , deplores the policy of racial discrimination and declares colonialism an evil that should be eradicated. Thus, political events and political ideas are closely related to Forster's moral ideas, which find their most profound expression in *A Passage to India*.

3. *Setting and Caves*

Forster's characters have a metaphysical as well as a physical relation to the setting, which both affects and reflects character, and is an active force in the novel. One is always aware of the weight of the climate, the shape of the land and the press of the crowd. Many of the chapters end with a meditative movement away from the characters to the setting that diminishes human endeavor in the vast perspective of unfathomed nature, and suggests reverberations of the infinite in the same way as do the conclusions of *Heart of Darkness* and *Nostromo*. The first chapter closes with the fists and fingers of the Marabar Hills; Godbole's song is followed by a moment of absolute and undisturbed silence; a game of patience ends with a description of the night sky and a warning of the approaching heat. Forster also relates setting to man by a personification of nature. The earth heaves and then lies flat, the hills creep near, and the hot weather advances like a swollen monster. Even the inhabitants of Chandrapore seem like mud moving.

Forster's Indian setting is anthropomorphic, exhibiting and reflecting itself according to the nature of the men who inhabit it. When man is evil, nature is evil; when man is harmonious, so nature is. The caves express in a forceful and energetic way the conflict between the two civilizations, and the racial and political hatred between Indians and English; and they figure forth in a horrible tableau the characters' inner states—Adela's anxieties about love, marriage and sex, and Mrs. Moore's doubts about religion. In the "Temple" section, where Indian and English are not hostile, nature becomes kind and snakes give way to water.

In "Wordsworth in the Tropics," Aldous Huxley shows the essential incompatibility between the idea of nature in English Romantic poetry and nature in the tropics that is "foreign, appalling, fundamentally and utterly inimical to intruding man."[41] Adela, who comes to grief in the Marabar Hills, does not realize this incompatibility, and as she approaches the caves that were thousands of miles from any scenery she understood, thinks of dearest Grasmere.

The English feel threatened by the power of India, and attempt to spread reason and orderliness in every direction. Their roads intersect at right angles, their bungalows form gridirons, and they intend to number the caves in sequence with white paint. Adela in particular hates mysteries, and relies on logic to explain the false dawn and the incident in the cave. She does not understand that the caves defy and deny reason, and does not, like Fielding, realize that clarity prevents spiritual intuition. The fieldglasses that Adela brings to the caves and breaks there, and that Aziz puts in his pocket, are in the tradition of the New Science, Newton's *Opticks* and eighteenth-century rationalism, and symbolize the futility of applying reason to the caves. Adela *quested* for the real India, but the country, like her gods, is not finite or unified. Like her gods, she speaks with a hundred voices in a hundred mouths. Like the green bird or the hairy animal, she cannot be labeled. Nothing in India is identifiable.

The anti-rational and elusive multifariousness of India is expressed in Forster's dualistic view of all experience in the novel. He continually emphasizes the need to see experience from two points of view and the need for a relative rather than an absolute judgment of human and even non-human behaviour. What appears to be one thing under western eyes is quite another to the Oriental vision. When Major Callendar calls Aziz away from his friends and then is not at home when Aziz arrives, the Indian considers it a spiteful and malicious show of power while the Englishman thinks he has been deliberately "let down" by a typically inefficient native subordinate. To Mrs Moore's "Oriental" mind, her meeting with Aziz in the mosque seems spontaneous and charming, while Ronny considers it quite an unpleasant scene. (Characteristically, Mrs Moore reconsidered the scene at the mosque, to see whose impression was correct.) The social misconceptions in the novel could be recounted at length by examining the eastern and western interpretation of why Aziz's collar stud popped out, why the Bhattacharyas failed to send their carriage, or why the Nawab Bahadur was so upset about a minor car accident. The rigid English interpretations, which refuse to consider the Indian viewpoint, are wrong in every instance. Even the echo, that turns all various sounds into the same monotonous noise, reflects the dualism of the "contradictory world."

These social misconceptions begin to take on ontological implications when the very nature of reality is questioned. What appears to be one thing often turns out to be something quite different, and the English can no longer be sure of what is real and what unreal. What caused the Nawab Bahadur's car accident? Was it the bridge, or the skid or a large animal? If an animal, was it a goat, or a buffalo or a hyena? With typical English calmness and reason Adela and Ronny trace the causal relationships and shine their torch on the car and road. "Steady and smooth ran the marks of the car, ribbons neatly nicked with lozenges, then *all went mad*. . . the torch created such high lights and black shadows that they *could not interpret* what it revealed"(89) (Italics mine).

The car accident prepares us for the psychological horror of the caves just as the Bridge Party and Fielding's tea party prepare us for the social disaster. (Ironically, Aziz wanted the trip to the caves to be a repetition of the tea party.) The car accident occurs on the Marabar road, the footholds of the caves remind Adela of the pattern of the Nawab Bahadur's car wheels, and Miss Derek arrives in her car after both accidents to rescue Adela.

Another important confusion of appearance and reality occurs en route to the caves.

> Miss Quested saw a thin, dark object reared on end at the farther side of the water-course, and said, "A snake!" The villagers agreed, and Aziz explained: yes, a black cobra, very venomous, who had reared himself up to watch the passing of the elephant. But when she looked through Ronny's field glasses, she found it wasn't a snake, but the withered and twisted stump of a toddy-palm. So she said, "It isn't a snake." The villagers contradicted her. She had put the word into their minds, and they refused to abandon it. Aziz admitted that it looked like a tree through the glasses, but insisted that it was a black cobra really . . . . Nothing was explained. (140-141)

It is very likely that Forster, so learned in Indian culture, was familiar with the writings of Samkara (8th century A.D.), the most famous authority on the *Vedanta*, the system of pantheistic philosophy based on the sacred literature of Hinduism, who

> explains the appearance of the world with an analogy. A person may mistake a rope for a serpent. The serpent is not there, but it is not entirely an illusion, for there is the rope. The appearance of the serpent lasts until the rope is closely examined. The world can be compared with the serpent and the *Brahman* with the rope. When we acquire true knowledge we recognize that the world is only a manifestation of the *Brahman*. The world is neither real nor quite unreal.[42]

The English generally mistake the illusory snake or world for the true reality, the "real India" that Adela longs to see, which is actually the rope or tree symbolizing the Brahman or spiritual essence.[43] They "would see India always as a frieze, never as a spirit"(47).

What Forster calls "rhythm", the use of repetition and variation to strike recurrent chords in the reader's mind, and which is expressed not only in the symbols and reverberating echoes but also in the overall cyclical pattern, is a structural as well as a thematic device. It is related to the seasonal cycle of each section (cool, hot and wet) and more importantly, to the dualistic scheme of the novel, for every important event has its necessary complement that reflects and enlarges its original meaning. Aziz tells Mrs Moore she is an Oriental and repeats the phrase to her son, which completes the cycle. There is the meeting in the mosque and the meeting on the maidan, an official Bridge Party and a private tea party, a Pathan tried for attempted rape by Ronny and an Indian tried for attempted rape by Das, an automobile accident involving the Nawab Bahadur, Adela and Ronny and one involving Nureddin and Aziz, a lift from Miss Derek after the first accident and after the cave episode, the festival of Mohurram and the festival of Gokul Ashtami, the chant of "Esmiss Esmoor" at the trial and the chant of "Radhakrishna, Radhakrishna" in Mau, the birth of Mrs Moore as a Hindu deity[44] and the birth of the deity Krishna at the Hindu festival, the release of the prisoner Aziz from the court after the trial and the release of the prisoner from the jail during the festival, the news of the death of Mrs Moore withheld during the Moslem "victory" celebrations and the news of the death of the Maharajah withheld during the Hindu religious celebrations.

A passage in one of Kipling's travel books is a literary source for the Marabar caves. Kipling's more explicit description is remarkable not only for its similarity to Forster's in its emphasis on the smoothness of the rocks and the darkness of the subterranean chamber, and its function as a symbol of "the soul of India", but also for the nightmarish apprehension of evil it inspires in the intruding visitor.

The stone of the steps had been worn and polished by the terrible naked feet till it showed its markings clearly as agate; and where the steps ended in a rock-slope, there was a visibie glair [sic] , a great snail-track, upon the rocks . . . .
Then he [Kipling] was conscious of remembering, with peculiar and unnecessary distinctness, that, from the Gau-Mukh, a passage led to the subterranean chambers . . . that some sort of devil, or ghoul, or Something, stood at the entrance of that approach. All of which was a nightmare bred in full day and folly to boot; but it was the fault of the Genius of the place, who made the Englishman feel that he had done a great wrong in trespassing into the very heart and soul of all Chitor. And, behind him, the Gau-Mukh gurgled and choked like a man in his death-throe. The Englishman endured as long as he could—about two minutes. Then it came upon him that he must go quickly out of this place of years and blood . . . and, above all, he did not care to look behind him, where stood the reminder that he was no better than the beasts that perish. But he had to cross the smooth, worn rocks, and he felt their sliminess through his boot soles . . . .
Perhaps it was absurd. It undoubtedly appeared so, later. Yet there was something uncanny about it all. It was not exactly a feeling of danger or pain, but an apprehension of great evil.[45]

the walls of the circular chamber had been most marvellously polished . . . Fists and fingers thrust above the advancing soil— here at last is their skin, finer than any covering acquired by the animals, smoother than windless water . . . They are dark caves. Even when they open towards the sun, very little light penetrates down the entrance tunnel into the circular chamber. (124–125).

Forster's subtle and superb description of the caves, of Chandrapore (which equals Conrad's portrayal of the Golfo Placido in the first pages of *Nostromo* for its brief but richly suggestive creation of an entire world and its enunciation of major themes), of the invasion of the heat, and of Mrs Moore's poetical farewell to India with its magnificently musical and Miltonic use of resonant place names — "the bilingual rock of Girnar, the statue of Shri Belgola, the ruins of Mandu and Hampi, temples of Khajraha, gardens of Shalimar" (210) —are among the finest passages in the modern English novel.

The geological genealogy of the hills and caves emphasizes their incredible antiquity with words like "prehistoric," "countless aeons," "primal," "sun's flesh," and "sun-born". They seem to belong to that time when "the earth was without form, and void, and darkness was upon the face of the deep," before the Spirit of God moved upon the face of the waters and said, "Let there be Light." The darkness of the caves is broken only by a flame and its reflection on the marvelously polished walls. "The two flames approach and strive to unite, but cannot, because one of them breathes air [the spiritual world], the other stone [the earthly world]." These flames, striving to unite, symbolize the sympathetic English and the Indians, Fielding and Aziz, Mrs Moore and Godbole. When Mrs Moore and Aziz meet in the mosque and begin their friendship, "The flame that not even beauty can nourish was springing up, and though his words were querulous his heart began to glow secretly . . . 'You understand me, you know what others feel.'" (23).

Another feature of the caves is their vacuity: nothing is inside them. "Nothing" is an extremely significant word in the novel, and Forster usually exploits both its meanings—no thing and nothingness— so that every statement using the word has a positive and a negative meaning. Professor Godbole says in his central speech, "everything is anything and nothing is something . . . absence is not non-existence" (178). Nothing (no thing) in India is identifiable because like the green bird and the hairy animal it refuses to be labeled; but nothingness *is* identifiable in the caves, with which the word is most frequently associated. When Mrs Moore realizes that the vile thing that struck her face in the cave was only a little baby, she says, "Nothing evil had been in the cave", that is, no evil thing but a vast and infinite nothingness that undermines the very foundation of her religious belief.

The caves are an active force that reshapes and redefines the lives of the characters who come into contact with them. The caves are a tenebrous immensity from which God's face is absent, an expression of a prehuman geological age. A malevolent spirit of perdition dwells within and causes Mrs Moore and Adela to experience pure abstract terror, sheer blank fright and cosmic rejection. The caves express a denial of western cultural values: clarity and form, rationalism, and the distinction between good and evil.

Though the experience in the cave is terrible, it is not entirely evil. Professor Godbole obliquely suggests that the dualistic knowledge of "good-and-evil" is synthesized in the cave episode when he tells Fielding

> When evil occurs, it expresses the whole of the universe. Similarly when good occurs . . . Good and evil are different, as their names imply. But, in my own humble opinion, they are both of them aspects of my Lord. He is present in the one, absent in the other, and the difference between presence and absence is great, as great as my feeble mind can grasp. Yet absence implies presence.[46] (178)

But Rose Macaulay ignores this central passage, sees the cave episode as totally evil and writes that the caves "land Aziz in prison, Adela in disgrace, Ronny in loneliness and bereavement, Fielding in embarrassments . . . [and] ruin Mrs Moore's health, temper and soul."[47]

But this interpretation is simplistic, for the cave experience, like Marlow's Congo journey, paradoxically brings forth good from evil. Except for Mrs Moore (who is later deified by the Indians), the ultimate effect of the cave episode is positive and enriching: and for Adela and Aziz, who are most deeply involved, the test of this experience leads to an awareness of their individual character and a new recognition of selfhood. (After the trial, "Adela was no longer examining life, but being examined by it; she had become a real person", (244–245)). The episode enables the characters to re-evaluate their lives and symbolizes the struggle of the individual towards the dark, secret place where he may find reality. Though the immediate and temporary effects seem evil, the episode prevents the loveless marriage between Ronny and Adela, unifies Hindus and Moslems in a common cause, provides a victory of the Indians over the English, vindicates the Indian character, demonstrates Indian integrity and ability in Judge Das, allows Aziz to regain his personal dignity and self-respect by escaping from British to Indian territory and rejoining his children, and deepens his friendship with Fielding and Godbole.

4.   *Temple and Hero*

Though Forster and Kipling differ about most things, they both prefer
Moslem clarity to Hindu confusion. Kipling writes, "I have never met
an Englishman yet who hated Islam and its people as I have met
Englishmen who hated some other faiths [i.e. Hinduism]. *Musalmani
awadani*, as the saying goes—where there are Mohammedans, there is a
comprehensible civilisation."[48] When Forster leaves the Hindu Native
State and meets his Moslem friend Masood, he notes, "I have passed
abruptly from Hinduism to Islam and the change is a relief. I have come
too into a world whose troubles and problems are intelligible to me".[49]

In his long humorous and ironic description of the ordered anarchy
in the Gokul Ashtami festival, Forster writes, "What troubles me is
that every detail, almost without exception, is fatuous and in bad
taste."[50] If Forster rejects the "nebulous story" of the birth at
Bethlehem, he is not likely to accept the Hindu legend with which he
compares it. Forster's essentially sceptical and rational cast of mind
invalidates Allen and Shahane's interpretation of the "Temple" section
as an expression of Hindu mystical union.[51] It would be more accurate
to emphasize the terrifying destructiveness of the echo than any
dubious claim of cosmic unity.

Throughout the book, Forster carefully prepares the reader for some
profound illumination in the "Temple" section by his consistent
metaphysical allusions (commonly associated with the elusive philosophy of the "inscrutable" Orient), and by his constant use of words
like "illusion", "spiritual", "premonition of eternity", "great distance",
"immense height", "whole universe", "infinite goal behind the stars",
and "shadow of a shadow of a dream"——which are deliberately
undercut by the anticlimax of a dull ordinary reality. (Even the
"Temple" section is anticlimactic to the exciting trial that takes place
in the middle part of the book.)

The terrifying echo, that strange penetrating antediluvian malevolence
rippling out of all the vanished spiteful eons, shatters and deranges
Mrs Moore, destroys her faith in religion and personal relationships,
and causes an extreme mental crisis. Yet the significance of the echo is
undermined as Mrs Moore sails from Bombay, for the Indian landscape
laughs mockingly and asks her, "'so you thought an echo was India;
you took the Marabar caves as final?'"(210).

Similarly when Mrs Moore experiences the "twilight of the double
vision," the extinction of the belief in transcendental worlds beyond
the earth, when she is about to communicate some profound truth

to us, Forster intrudes with "Visions are *supposed* to entail profundity, but—Wait till you get one, dear Reader! The abyss also may be petty, the serpent of eternity made of maggots" (208) (Italics mine). And right after Professor Godbole sings his mystifying song to Krishna who neglects to come, Ronny's clerk Krishna, "the peon who should have brought the files from his office . . . *had not turned up,* and a terrific row ensued" (97) (Italics mine). This is pure comedy and pulls the carpet from under us while we ponder the mysteries of Godbole's song.

In the same way, the collision of the boats in the Tank at Mau, narrated by Forster with gusto, sly amusement and a farfetched simile, is a comical comment on the theme of unity and the impossibility of achieving it other than through the unexpected—and wet— physical jolt into the "Indian element."

> The four outsiders flung out their arms and grappled, and, with oars and poles sticking out, revolved like a mythical monster in the whirlwind. The worshippers howled with wrath *or* joy, as they drifted forward helplessly . . . [Stella] flung herself against Aziz and her motions capsized them. They plunged into the warm, shallow water, and rose struggling into a tornado of noise. The oars, the sacred tray, the letters of Ronny and Adela, broke loose and floated confusedly. Artillery was fired, drums beaten, the elephants trumpeted, and *drowning* all an immense peal of thunder, unaccompanied by lightning, cracked like a mallet on the dome.
> This was the climax, *as far as India admits of one* (315) (Italics mine).

This scene makes one feel like the spectators after the birth of the god; though the revelation was over, everyone felt it had not yet come.

Professor Godbole is the embodiment of the elusive quality of Hinduism: "Study it for years with the best teachers, and when you raise your head, nothing they have told you quite fits . . . no man could say where was the emotional centre of it, any more than he could locate the heart of a cloud" (292, 396). Godbole possesses the knack of slipping off, and though his name suggests openness and bounty (God's bowl) and means "sweet-tongued" in Hindi, he has never told anyone anything. Though elusive, he is a positive force in the novel and expresses the Forsterian ideal of a harmony that reconciled the products of East and West and could never be discomposed. It is no accident that "he neglects to come" and that his protracted prayers make him miss the train to the caves, which symbolize the separation of men and the chaos that results from this lack of harmony.

Reverberations of the Professor's celebrated song echo throughout the novel. Krishna refuses to come to the milkmaiden who beseeches him to come to her only, because her request is selfish and exclusive (like the English missionaries who live near the slaughterhouse that profanes the Hindu religion) and is contrary to the basic tenets of Hinduism: the belief in the deep accord and fellowship with *all* things on earth. The selfless punkah-wallah who sends air to others, and receives none himself, is the opposite of the egocentric and demanding milkmaiden.

The god does come in the Gokul Ashtami festival after Godbole invokes Tukaram, the greatest mystic saint of the Maharashtra and the exponent of the union with God through love. Godbole, for whom religion is a living force,

> had once more developed the life of his spirit. He had, with increasing vividness, again seen Mrs Moore, and round her faintly clinging forms of trouble. He was a Brahman, she Christian, but it made no difference, it made no difference whether she was a trick of his memory or a telepathic appeal. It was his duty, as it was his desire, to place himself in the position of the God and to love her, and to place himself in her position and to say to the God, 'Come, come, come. come'. (290-291)

By interceding for Mrs Moore Godbole places himself in a spiritual state in which he is worthy of receiving the god of infinite Love, and illustrates Forster's belief that "Religion is more than an ethical code with a divine sanction. It is also a means through which man may get into direct contact with the divine."[52] Godbole expresses the theme of *desired* unity that Forster has taken from Whitman's "Passage to India":

> Lo, soul, sees't thou not God's purpose from the first?
> The earth to be spann'd, connected by network,
> The races, neighbors, to marry and be given in marriage,
> The oceans to be cross'd, the distant brought near,
> The lands to be welded together.

The opposite of this is the emotional and religious sterility of modern man (exemplified by the English officials), which is expressed in Eliot's "The Waste Land":

I can connect
Nothing with Nothing.

If Godbole embodies the theme of unity in the spiritual realm, Fielding embodies it on the personal level. Fielding, of course, is very like Forster and possesses the personal, social and moral qualities that Forster has praised in his non-fiction. Like Forster, Fielding is humane, intellectually curious and liberal. Fielding is an exception to the rule that "The English always stick together!", for he defends Aziz against the uniform opposition of the entire club, and ostracizes himself from the English community by staking his reputation and integrity on his friend's innocence. Fielding has tolerance, good temper and sympathy, and can put himself in another person's place. Though "it is impossible to regard a tragedy from two points of view" (165), Fielding tries to do so when Aziz is accused. He has a strong feeling of common humanity and strives for a union of perfect equality with people of different races. Unlike all the other Englishmen, he rejects the Sahib's role, and is not corrupted by officialism or by life in the tropics. Fielding's first appearance in the novel is very brief but characteristic. When Adela asks how to see the "real India," he suggests that she try seeing Indians. After Aziz is freed, he tells Adela he is happy and secure in India, that he likes the people and has earned their trust. Fielding believes men can communicate with each other through good will, culture and intelligence.

In spite of Fielding's noblest efforts, friendship fails at the end of *A Passage to India* because men cannot be friends without being equals: politics precludes friendship. The possibilities of friendship are tested and fail in 1924, with the hope that they will develop in a future and happier time, and that the final "No, not yet", can be transcended. A passage to India in Whitman's sense, "All these separations and gaps shall be taken up and hook'd and link'd together", *is* made by Fielding, so that positive hopes are sounded amidst disappointment and despair.

3

JOSEPH CONRAD:
THE MEANING OF
CIVILIZATION

KIPLING and Conrad were the only great authors who wrote of imperialism during the zenith of its power and influence, and both derived a breadth and vitality from their colonial experience that surpassed all of their pre-War contemporaries. Because of Conrad's unfamiliar subject matter and exotic settings, and his concern with devotion to duty and self-discipline, his first critics labelled him a spinner of sea yarns and the Kipling of the Malay Archipelago. Conrad disliked these epithets and wrote that he hoped "to get freed from that infernal tail of ships and that obsession of my sea life... I do wish that all those ships of mine were given a rest."[1] And in the last year of his life Conrad was still defending stories like "Youth" and "Typhoon" against the inappropriate tag. Conrad justly thought his works were more ambitious and profound than Kipling's and resented the comparison with him. Comparing his own works with Kipling's Conrad writes that "Un écrivain *national* comme Kipling par exemple traduit facilement. Son intérêt est *dans le sujet*, l'intérêt de mon oeuvre est *dans l'effet* qu'elle produit. Il parle de ses *compatriotes*. Moi j'écris *pour eux*."[2]

Carrington's statement that "Conrad visited Kipling at 'Bateman's' [Kipling's home in Sussex] and each was an admirer of the other's work"[3] needs some qualification. Though Conrad calls attention to Kipling's works in a letter to his Polish cousin, he expresses serious, if somewhat cryptic, reservations about Kipling's work in two letters to his friend Cunninghame Graham:

Mr. Kipling has the wisdom of the passing generations,— and holds it in perfect sincerity. Some of his work is of impeccable form and because of that *little* thing, he will sojourn in Hell only a very short while. He squints with the rest of his excellent sort.

You understood perfectly what I tried to say about Mr. Kipling,—

but I did not succeed in saying exactly what I wanted to say. I wanted to say, in effect, that in the chaos of printed matter Kipling's *ébauches* appear by contrast finished and impeccable. I judge the man in his time, —and space. It is a small space and as to his time I leave it to your tender mercy. I wouldn't in his defence spoil the small amount of steel that goes to the making of a needle.[4]

Conrad seems to be chiding Kipling for his irritating precocious knowingness and the shallowness and limitations of his moral vision, while granting that he is superior to his rather undistinguished contemporaries.

But it was Kipling's political attitudes that were most offensive to Conrad as well as to Forster, for Conrad writes of the Boer War, "There is an appalling fatuity in this business. If I am to believe Kipling this is a war undertaken for the cause of democracy. *C'est à crêver de rire!*"[5] And Conrad used to shock Ford "by declaring that the French were the only European nation who knew how to colonise; they had none of the spirit of Mr. Kipling's 'You Bloody-niggerisms' about them."[6] Retinger is therefore more accurate than Carrington when he maintains that Conrad "had the prejudice of many of his contemporaries against what they called Kipling's reporter style and his 'journalese' ...Conrad never understood the great Imperialist, and, indeed, disliked him intensely."[7]

Conrad's attitudes are closer to Forster than to Kipling; the Marabar caves and the heart of darkness, Fielding and Marlow, have much in common.[8] But the differences between the setting and society of India and the Congo and South America suggest some contrasts between Forster and Conrad. In India there are ancient religions and glorious civilizations, which are celebrated by Aziz who aspires to emulate his Moghul ancestors. India has sophisticated, articulate, elegant and cultured natives — Professor Godbole, the Nawab Bahadur and Dr Aziz — who are intellectual companions of those English who care to cultivate their friendship. In India there is the natural rhythm of seasonal variations so that the awful intensity of the heat is followed by the welcome respite of the rains.

Neither the Congo nor Costaguana have these characteristics. The heart of darkness is a dominating and immediate presence, and the "fascination of the abomination" carries a forceful and overwhelming threat. The Africans of the jungle and the Indians of the Campo are either violent and dangerous or squalid and oppressed, and there is little opportunity for meaningful personal intercourse with them. The influence of coastal civilization on natives like Bento and Sotillo has merely intensified their brutality. And there is no relief from the extreme horror of the Congo, which Conrad paints in the most sombre colours.

A second important difference between Forster and Conrad is that *A Passage to India* is philosophical and speculative, and seriously considers questions of metaphysics and religion. This difference is reflected in Fielding and Marlow: the former is a highly educated and cultured teacher, who has probably known something of Cambridge and Bloomsbury; while the latter is a man of action, a sailor of the eastern seas and a ship's captain.

Heart of Darkness (1899) and *Nostromo* (1904) have some important similarities and can be discussed together profitably. Though one work is set in central Africa and the other in South America, both settings are characterized by a gloomy and brooding darkness that symbolizes moral blindness as well as the hidden evil in man. Both places are unusually isolated and inaccessible, the sources of great rivers and great wealth, inhabited by savages less ferocious and corrupt than the white men who rule the country. Both places stand completely outside the conventions and norms of European civilization. The settings are violently hostile to man and express the immense indifference of things that swallows up Kurtz and Decoud. The conclusions of both works reflect Conrad's most vital style, powerfully evoke the setting and mood, and universalize the themes by relating them to the vastness of the sea and the sky.

> The offing was barred by a black bank of clouds, and the tranquil waterway leading to the uttermost ends of the earth flowed somber under an overcast sky— seemed to lead into the heart of an immense darkness.

> In that true cry of undying passion that seemed to ring aloud from Punta Mala to Azuera and away to the bright line of the horizon, overhung by a big white cloud shining like a mass of solid silver, the genius of the magnificent capataz de cargadores dominated the dark gulf containing his conquests of treasure and love.

The imperialistic manifestation of the remote European civilization,

a crass material progress without any corresponding moral values, is
totally destructive and fails terribly in both the Congo and Costaguana.
Conrad believes that civilization can flourish only when it is carefully
nourished and guarded by a few select men (somewhat like Stendhal's
"Happy Few") who remain faithful to their code of honor. It cannot
be transplanted and cannot survive in remote places where great
temptation and danger exist. *Heart of Darkness* and *Nostromo* both
show how the evil and corrupt side of man betrays his civilized ideals.

Various characters in *Nostromo* develop and expand aspects of
Kurtz's character. Like Kurtz, Gould abandons his beloved, and
becomes isolated and doomed in remote regions. Decoud disintegrates
in the wilderness, as Kurtz does, because he lacks the inner strength
to face the utter solitude. And Nostromo's reputation is also slowly and
carefully established and then suddenly destroyed. Both men are
represented by the material wealth that corrupts them: Kurtz by his
ivory skull and Nostromo by his silver horse and buttons.

1.   *Heart of Darkness*

Heart of Darkness reveals that the interests of civilization and colonization are basically antagonistic, and asks the central questions about
this conflict: what happens to the civilized white man and to the
African when they clash? and what values does the European need
to survive this conflict? Marlow, a most discreet, understanding man,
has integrity, tolerance, and compassion, and these qualities sustain
him in the Congo. He comes to Africa with a strong moral sense and
remains faithful to his ideas throughout his nightmarish journey.
Marlow represents the European conscience that Kurtz has abandoned
somewhere in the interior of the jungle, and his behavior and
condemnation of the colonial venture reaffirm the values of civilization.

The most significant concept in Marlow's moral system is faithfulness
to the moral idea, which is contrasted to sentimental pretence and
false principles. What redeems the conquest of the earth is an unselfish
belief in the idea, a sense of innate strength and individual will, and
power of devotion to a just cause. Marlow is the only person in *Heart
of Darkness* who remains loyal to these ideals.

The sentimental pretence and false principles are held by the
rapacious hypocrites in Brussels, who would disguise their true motives
with high-sounding phrases and philanthropic pretence and turn

Marlow into an apostolic emissary of light; by the naive and trustful innocents, like Marlow's aunt and Kurtz's intended, who get carried away by that humbug and speak of educating those horrid and ignorant millions; and even by that sometime idealist Kurtz, who was destroyed by the Congo, so pitiless to human weakness.

Marlow is careful to avoid the frightening reality that is impenetrable to human thought through his dedication to work. In *Heart of Darkness,* work does not have the absolute value that it had for the simpler heroes, like Captain MacWhirr, in Conrad's sea tales. Now, work is not an end in itself but rather a means of survival, a mode of distraction. Through work Marlow hides the inner truth, the dread reality, and keeps hold on the redeeming facts of life.

As Marlow slowly steams into the Congo, he passes out of a familiar world and into a strange one. The first world, as he tells his listeners late in the story, is one in which a man is subject to external restraints and firmly *moored*, "like a hulk with two anchors, [with] a butcher round one corner, a policeman round another, excellent appetites, and temperature normal".[9] In the world of the heart of darkness, men "were cut off from the comprehension of their surroundings . . . The earth seemed unearthly. We are accustomed to look upon the shackled form of a conquered monster, but there— there you could look at the thing monstrous and free"(256). Work serves the dual function of hiding the "inner truth" of the heart of darkness, and absorbing Marlow in the "surface truth" that keeps him moored to the familiar world.[10] Marlow's need for work is symbolized in his search for rivets that will hold himself as well as the tin-pot steamboat together. Unlike Decoud in *Nostromo* who lost all belief in the reality of his action and went mad in the utter silence and utter solitude of unfamiliar nature, Marlow understands that "In our activity alone do we find the sustaining illusion of an independent existence as against the whole scheme of things of which we form a helpless part . . . Only in the conduct of our action can we find the sense of mastery over the Fates."[11] This is what Marlow means by the chance to find yourself and your own reality.

One of Marlow's great qualities is that he measures his colonial experience in human and moral terms. Unlike Kurtz, he is dubious about the idea of progress and sceptical about what civilization can do for the Africans, and he clearly recognizes that colonialism, at least as it is practised in the Congo, is a totally destructive process. Though Marlow certainly shares Kurtz's fascination with the mysteries of the Congo, he harbors no idealistic illusions about his "mission" and has no desire to suppress savage customs. Marlow is scornful of the white men he meets, deliberately alienates himself from them, and remains solitary and aloof on his boat. But he does commit himself— emotionally and compassionately—to the Africans he encounters throughout his journey. Their suffering reflects the white man's cruel visitation just as their honorable restraint represents a moral standard that the Europeans fail to meet.

Marlow's first contact with Africans on the west coast is the only positive experience of the entire story, and the only one with a universal validity outside the unnatural, absurd and unreal Congo.

> Now and then a boat from the shore gave one a momentary contact with reality. It was paddled by black fellows. You could see from afar the white of their eyeballs glistening. They shouted, sang; their bodies streamed with perspiration; they had faces like grotesque masks—these chaps; but they had bone, muscle, a wild vitality, an intense energy of movement, that was as natural and true as the surf along their coast. They wanted no excuse for being there. They were a great comfort to look at. For a time I would feel I belonged still to a world of straight-forward facts; but the feeling would not last long. Something would turn up to scare it away. (229–230)

This physical energy and spiritual vitality is the familiar norm that Marlow recognizes and understands, and that is degraded, perverted and corrupted by tropical enervation and human brutality.

Each stage in Marlow's journey is marked by vicious cruelties to Africans that the whites attempt to justify by false accusations and misleading epithets. The incomprehensible French man-of-war firing into a continent is followed by the railroad chain gang of doomed human slaves being driven by a Europeanized African, the product of the new forces at work[12]. The men dying slowly in the grove of death were neither enemies nor criminals:

> they were nothing earthly now—nothing but black shadows of disease and starvation . . . Brought from all recesses of the coast in all the legality of time contracts, lost in uncongenial surroundings, fed on unfamiliar food, they sickened, became inefficient, and were then allowed to crawl away and rest . . . The black bones reclined at full length with one shoulder against

the tree, and slowly the eyelids rose and the sunken eyes looked
up at me, enormous and vacant, a kind of blind, white flicker
in the depths of the orbs, which died out slowly. (233-234)

The vital Africans on the coast and these *moribundi* in the grove of
death are like the two side panels in a medieval triptych of the last
Judgment where the damned are cast down and the saved raised up.
Marlow perceives these two worlds with an extraordinary awareness and
with a strange feeling of detachment. Like the white men and the
coastal natives, these black shadows of disease are strangers to the
interior and cannot withstand the agonies they suffer.

As Marlow continues to penetrate the interior, the Africans—
targets, slaves, skeletons, corpses and victims — mark the stages of his
via dolorosa. He stumbles over the body of a murdered African, and
encounters another innocent who is being horribly flogged and who soon
disappears into the wilderness, presumably to die there.

The final and most ghastly horror that Marlow encounters is the
black dried human heads that decorate Kurtz's fence, and Marlow
darkly suggests that these victims of "unspeakable rites" might have
been human sacrifices devoured by cannibals. As the power of the
whites becomes absolute, the torments inflicted upon the Africans
become more extreme, until they foreshadow the greater horrors of
the twentieth century.

Marlow's encounters with the Africans are painful, and his meetings
with the Europeans are disillusioning, for almost all of them are as
hollow as Kurtz. The bookkeeper has survived the jungle by imposing
an absolute order on his immediate surroundings; the manager by
absolute health, leaving his entrails in Europe, as it were; the brickmaker by backbiting and intriguing; and the young Russian by partaking
in naive adventures that sustain him in unreality. All of these alternatives
fail because they are imposed externally and superficially, for in the
Congo a man must meet the destructive chaos with his own true stuff
and inborn strength. This is impossible for them because, unlike
Marlow, they have no true stuff. The accountant is like a hairdresser's
dummy; the manager has nothing within him; the brickmaker is a
papier-mâché Mephistopheles. The Russian is not hollow but merely a
fool, appropriately dressed in motley. In contrast to the man of true
stuff, the fool with his frightened gapes and shudders is always safe
because he is too dull to realize he is being assaulted by the powers of
darkness.

The Europeans' treatment of the Africans and their own corrupt values alienate Marlow from his fellow whites. He is outraged by his inability to prevent their inhumanity, even aboard his own ship, and ashamed of his complicity in the guilt of the Belgian company. This intensifies his isolation and his need for human contact; his sense of the absurd and the incomprehensible; and his desire to meet Kurtz. Marlow assumes that Kurtz shares his values, understands the Congo and can somehow explain the unreal to him, can give him the human contact and stabilizing influence he so badly needs, and can share the loneliness of his thoughts. But when he is confronted with Kurtz, he feels disappointment, resentment, anger and fear. He faces reality for the first time, looks into Kurtz's mad soul, suffers a moral shock, breaks down, and nearly dies.

The only human relationship Marlow is able to establish is with his African helmsman.

> It was a kind of partnership. He steered for me— I had to look after him. I worried about his deficiencies, and thus a subtle bond had been created, of which I only became aware when it was suddenly broken.[13] And the intimate profundity of that look he gave me when he received his hurt remains to this day in my memory—like a claim of distant kinship affirmed in a supreme moment. (274)

This kinship, like the one between Rudbeck and Mister Johnson, evolves when men work together and realize the need for human solidarity against a hostile natural world. Marlow believes in "the subtle but invincible conviction of solidarity that knits together the loneliness of innumerable hearts, the solidarity in dreams, in joy, in sorrow, in aspirations, in illusions, in hope, in fear, which binds men to each other, which binds together all humanity".[14]

Marlow's kinship with the helmsman suggests his relationship both to Africans and to Kurtz. His look of intimate profundity recalls the enormous and vacant stare of the dying man in the grove of death and links the helmsman with the other African victims. And Marlow's subtle bond and distant kinship foreshadows his close relationship with Kurtz, who, like the helmsman, had no restraint.

Ironically, the only men in the tale who do show restraint, except for Marlow himself, are his cannibalistic crew. These cannibals, paid with brass wire and fed on scanty rations of rotten hippo meat, are slowly starving. The stench of the rotten hippo, which the pilgrims cannot get rid of though they throw most of it overboard, is Conrad's metaphor for the corruption in the Congo. Marlow exclaims that "You can't breathe dead hippo waking, sleeping, and eating, and at the same time keep your precarious grip on existence," yet this is precisely what he is forced to do: "breathe dead hippo, so to speak, and not be contaminated" (262, 273).

These cannibals, like Montaigne's, have a code of primitive honor, and the inborn strength to fight hunger properly; and though Marlow considers their behavior an unfathomable enigma, he compares it to the foam on the depths of the sea that seemed natural and true when the vital African boatmen rode through it on the coast. The cannibals, still powerful and muscular despite starvation, are strangers to the inner reaches of the Congo, and Marlow associates them with the men of bone, muscle, and wild vitality who dwell on the coast. Unlike the whites, the stoical crew have imposed self-restraint and maintained their code of honor amidst the heart of darkness, and their behavior denies any European claim of superior civilization. The crew are a strong contrast to Kurtz's adorers, primitives corrupted by a civilizing mission, whose savage clamor broke the silence of the jungle.

The respective roles of Marlow and Kurtz have been foreshadowed by their imperialistic Roman prototypes as well as by their African followers. Like Marlow, the trireme commander is revolted by the marshes, forests, savages and wilderness at the very end of the world, does not go ashore, and is man enough to face the darkness. By contrast, the paradigm for Kurtz is the citizen in a toga who does go ashore and feels the utter savagery had encircled him. He feels "The fascination of the abomination. . . the growing regrets, the longing to escape, the powerless disgust, the surrender, the hate" (221). Like the other Europeans, Kurtz lacks inborn strength and preys on others' weaknesses, and the wilderness echoes loudly within him because he is hollow at the core.

The fate of those who feel the fascination of the abomination is a central question in the story, and is asked by the company doctor in Brussels and by the Swedish captain in Africa. Marlow, noting the changes in himself as well as in others, becomes increasingly concerned with his ability to survive the heart of darkness. Though Marlow's actual experience in the Congo is negative, he is able to handle it successfully, and it has a positive effect on him by strengthening his moral awareness. For Marlow the jungle is a menace, for Kurtz it is an appeal, and the first chapter closes with Marlow asking about the fate of Kurtz in the Congo.

Like the brilliant and tragic Rimbaud, Kurtz was a poet and idealist who came to grief in the African wilderness, and Rimbaud's letter from Abyssinia in 1888 expresses what Kurtz must have suffered before Marlow found him:

> I am lonely and bored. I have never known anyone as lonely and bored as I. Is it not wretched, this life I lead, without family, without friends, without any intellectual companionship or occupation, lost in the midst of these negroes, whose lot one would like to improve and who try, for their part, to exploit you . . . Obliged to chatter their jibberish, to eat their filthy messes, to endure a thousand and one annoyances that come from their idleness, their treachery, and their stupidity. But that is not the worst. The worst thing is the fear of becoming dotish oneself, isolated as one is, and cut off from any intellectual companionship.[15]

And Kurtz's long isolation in the wilderness awakens the memory of savage passions, of forgotten and brutal instincts, which Thoreau also experienced:

> I caught a glimpse of a woodchuck stealing across my path, and felt a strange thrill of savage delight, and I was strongly tempted to seize and devour him raw; not that I was hungry then, except for that wilderness which he represented . . . I found myself ranging the woods, like a half-starved hound, with a strange abandonment, seeking some kind of venison which I might devour, and no morsel could have been too savage for me.[16]

But Kurtz, unlike Thoreau, eventually succumbs to madness: the wilderness got into his "veins, consumed his flesh, and sealed his soul to its own by the inconceivable ceremonies of some devilish initiation" (271). Conrad thus reverses the myth of isolated man's conquest of wild nature, established by *Robinson Crusoe,* for our century, unlike the eighteenth, recognizes the power of the wilderness to liberate the evil instincts in man. Kurtz loses his spiritual belief, his moral sense, and his reason as well, the very qualities that distinguish man from beasts.

If, as Jung says, the growth of civilization and culture consists "in a progressive subjugation of the animal in man" ("the shackled form of a conquered monster"), then Kurtz's deterioration represents a "rebellion on the part of the animal nature that thirsts for freedom"[17] ("a thing monstrous and free"), and the chaos and aggression that result when civilized man gives way to his instinctual impulses.[18] "Separation from his instinctual nature," Jung writes, "inevitably plunges civilized man into the conflict between conscious and unconscious, spirit and nature, knowledge and faith, a split that becomes pathological the moment his consciousness is no longer able to neglect or suppress his instinctual side."[19] The dominance of Kurtz's instincts over his conscious will and his surrender to the wilderness symbolize a reversal of the idea of progress and a return of the "universal genius" of modern man to the brutal barbarity and moral anarchy represented in *Heart of Darkness* by the ancient Britons. Kurtz's condemnation, the terse but richly ambiguous "The horror! The horror!," expresses at once a significant truth about himself and about the heart of darkness that has eclipsed the civilized side of his personality. Kurtz's attempt to civilize the Africans was a triumph over the instinctual impulse—over the shadow of the great forest. To kill them was an attempt to kill this impulse.

Despite Kurtz's monstrous brutality that was responsible for the ornamental heads of human sacrifices, and the fact that he is the very embodiment and cause of the horrors Marlow has witnessed, Marlow is able to pronounce Kurtz's eternal condemnation, "an affirmation, a moral victory paid for by innumerable defeats, by abominable terrors, by abominable satisfactions. But it was a victory! . . . his magnificent eloquence [was] thrown to me from a soul as translucently pure as a cliff of crystal" (299). Marlow finds Kurtz's forthright evil more palatable than his colleagues' corrupt hypocrisy and devious villainy, and remains faithful to his "choice of nightmares". Knowing the worst about Kurtz and through Kurtz about the evil in himself and all men, Marlow admires Kurtz's struggle for moral awareness and self-knowledge in the face of an overwhelming assault by the powers of darkness.

Yet Marlow is no longer able to judge Kurtz's final cry. Like the other white men and the Africans who have been transformed from vital and energetic coastal men into listless corpses in the grove of death, Marlow has been severely affected by the jungle. (When Marlow returns to Brussels he ironically says that Kurtz's end was in every way worthy of his life.) Though Marlow does not realize it, he too has become unmoored and has lost his precarious grip on reality. He has been suffering continuously from fever and chills, and he now suffers something like a nervous breakdown, the result of a diseased imagination, and wrestles with death.

Marlow has suffered with Kurtz, and his mental strain has been

even greater than his physical one, for Marlow had to go through the
ordeal of looking into Kurtz's mad soul. "I saw the inconceivable
mystery of a soul that knew no restraint, no faith, and no fear, yet
struggling blindly with itself. I kept my head pretty well... while my
legs shook under me.... It is *his* extremity that I seem to have lived
through. True, he had made that last stride, he had stepped over the
edge, while I had been permitted to draw back my hesitating foot.
And perhaps this is the whole difference" (294, 299). This difference
is Marlow's conscience and moral ideas that enable him to withdraw
from the abyss as Kurtz plunges into it.[20]

Marlow believes that Kurtz ultimately achieved self-knowledge,
and through his human commitment to Kurtz he is able to share his
self-knowledge as he had shared his pain. This self-awareness is the
only positive result of Marlow's Congo experience, and is revealed
in the insights he is able to communicate as he tells the story, relives
his experience and deepens his understanding.

Marlow has been mentally and morally transformed by his journey.
"Going up that river was like travelling back to the earliest beginnings
of the world . . . you thought yourself bewitched and cut off for ever
from everything you had known once — somewhere — far away — in
another existence perhaps . . . We were wanderers on a prehistoric earth,
on an earth that wore the aspect of an unknown planet . . . we were
travelling in the night of first ages, of those ages that are gone, leaving
hardly a sign — and no memories" (253-256). Marlow has discovered
that the heart of darkness and the potentiality for corruption and evil
lie within every man, no matter how civilized, that the possibilities of
reversion to primitive savagery (of ancient Britain and the Congo) exist,
and that the good man needs immense resources to resist the fascination
of the abomination. His identification with Kurtz after his journey into
self is a recognition of his own frailty.

Conrad, with his three languages, two nationalities and two
professions, was intensely aware of his own dual character and obsessed
with the problem of identity and selfhood. He refers to himself as "a
Polish gentleman, cased in British tar!"[21] and says "Le 'homo duplex'
a, de mon cas, plus d'un sens."[22] And in his greatest fiction, most
obviously in "The Secret Sharer", *The Shadow-Line* and *Lord Jim,*
but also in *Heart of Darkness* and *Nostromo,* Conrad considers the
theme of the potentially evil other self.

Marlow's identification with Kurtz makes him decide to visit
Kurtz's intended. Conrad felt this scene was extremely important
and wrote to William Blackwood: "in the light of the final incident,

the whole story in all its descriptive detail shall fall into its place —
acquire its value and its significance."[23] Like Marlow's aunt, the
intended possesses a saving illusion and is completely out of touch
with truth. The atrocious phantom Kurtz had demanded justice on
his deathbed but Marlow, the secret sharer of his guilt, remains loyal
and gives him mercy. Marlow realizes that certain terrible truths must
be kept hidden, and that men must help women to preserve the
saving illusion and to remain in their own beautiful world "lest ours
get worse". He wisely protects the intended from unnecessary pain by
allowing her to maintain her ideal vision of Kurtz, although it involves
a hateful lie. When Marlow moves from an absolute to a relative
standard of behavior (this has already been suggested by his choice
of nightmares), he reveals a new awareness of evil in the world, and
successfully readjusts to the European norm.[24]

Marlow is Conrad's literary resolution of the problem of the other
self, for he is sensitive to both good and evil and perceives their
interaction in human life. His moral sense, imagination, scepticism,
self-doubts, and especially his dual vision of reality, enable him to
embrace both worlds and to interpret the primeval horrors of the heart
of darkness.

2.   Nostromo

In *Nostromo*, as in *Heart of Darkness*, Conrad takes great care to
contrast the familiar European world, what Forster calls "the Mediterranean norm", with the savage and ferocious Costaguana, whose coast
had never been ruled by the gods of Olympus; where everything
merely rational fails. Only the marble statue of King Carlos IV is
able to preserve its steady, passionless, European poise. The more
corporeal Europeans are all uneasy and frightened, possessed by a
strange feeling of unreality. In the wilds of Costaguana, Sir John
utterly lost touch with the feeling of European life; and Dr Monygham's
tortures did away with his Europeanism. Mrs Gould concealed her
deep dismay at the remote and unfamiliar conventions; and Charles
Gould too was deeply disturbed "by that parody of civilized institutions
which offended his intelligence, his uprightness, and his sense of
right.... The words one knows so well," he says, "have a nightmarish
meaning in this country. Liberty, democracy, patriotism, government —

all of them have a flavour of folly and murder" (304, 327). This sense of unreality, the fear and the lack of absolute values, make the characters particularly vulnerable, and force them to cling to the tangible silver for their security and salvation.

The violent spirit of Costaguana, so different from the placidity of its somber gulf, is expressed most forcefully in the treacherous anarchy and savage chaos of its history, which is nothing more than "fifty years of misrule". The brutal torment of Don José Avellanos and the ghastly torture of Dr Monygham are testaments to the somber imbecility of political fanaticism with which Guzmán Bento tyrannized the country. The startling description in the opening chapter of the enlightened Ribiera and his followers fleeing for their lives before the Monterist Revolution is a potent warning about the fate of progressive governments in Costaguana. The history of the country, cruel ferocity linked with poverty and oppression, is symbolized by the huge iron spurs fastened to the naked heels of the soldiers.

Into this milieu the Europeans attempt to introduce progress, which as Conrad says, "leaves its dead by the way, for progress is only a great adventure as its leaders and chiefs know very well in their hearts. It is a march into an undiscovered country; and in such an enterprise the victims do not count."[25] The deep sea galleons of the Spanish conquerors, who were attracted by the wealth of Costaguana three hundred years before, have been replaced by the clipper ships of the modern imperialists who continue the exploitation. Whereas the Spanish created an ecclesiastical court and two vice-royalties, the modern financiers offer steamers, a railway, and a telegraph, which they believe is worth infinitely more than the ecclesiastical past. This crucial judgment, though upheld by Gould in his "material interests" speech, is ultimately disproved by the events of the novel. The history of the Gould Concession shows that civilized values are destroyed, not created, by material interests.

The effect of the railway, the telegraph and the mine on the life of the country is not so beneficial as the financiers imagine. The rattling noise of the mine's ore shoots is like the shrieking ghost of a railway engine that startles the silent movement of the people on the road. The railway's chain-couplings and fetters recall the shackles of José Avellanos in the chain gang and the bondage of Costaguana under Bento, and suggest that the railroad, whose terrible noise frightens the people and disturbs the timeless silence of the campo, is a new and more insidious form of enslavement. And the serpentine telegraph, like a ghastly garrotte, twines itself about the weary heart of the land. The delusive promises of the financiers are understandably received with sceptical reserve by the rancheros of the campo who refuse to sell their land to the railroad.

The history of the mine reflects the history of the country. Like the old Spanish bridges and churches, the yield of the mine had been paid for with the weight of human bones. In the time of Gould's father, it was a wild, inaccessible, and rocky gorge strewn with refuse and tailings. In Charles Gould's day the mine continues to disfigure nature and destroy the traditional life of the people, a terrible penalty for progress that does not bring permanent security.

Emilia Gould, whose watercolor sketch preserves the ruined waterfall and who recalls the glories of the vice-regal past to Sir John, is shocked at the changes. She wishes to preserve the simple and picturesque aspects of traditional rural life, and the great worth of the suffering and patient people. Emilia's vision of the tranquil rhythms of the ageless life in the plains and the mountains is destined to extinction by "The material apparatus of perfected civilization which obliterates the individuality of old towns under the stereotyped conveniences of modern life" (89), which abolishes the popular feasts and undermines the religion, the very sources of cultural and spiritual vitality in the painful and penurious life of the people.

> She saw them on the road carrying loads, lonely figures upon the plain, toiling under great straw hats, with their white clothing flapping about their limbs in the wind; she remembered the villages by some group of Indian women at the fountain impressed upon her memory, by the face of some young Indian girl with a melancholy and sensual profile, raising an earthenware vessel of cool water at the door of a dark hut with a wooden porch cumbered with great brown jars. The solid wooden wheels of an oxcart, halted with its shafts in the dust, showed the strokes of the axe; and a party of charcoal carriers, with each man's load resting above his head on the top of the low mud wall, slept stretched in a row within the strip of shade. (84)

Don Pepe, Viola, Decoud, Nostromo, and even Gamacho, all testify to the oppression and exploitation that is the inevitable lot of the people. Emilia Gould "saw the San Tomé mountain hanging over the campo, over the whole land, feared, hated, wealthy—more soulless than any tyrant, more pitiless and autocratic than the worst government,

ready to crush innumerable lives in the expansion of its greatness"
(414).26

The silver of the mine is the symbol of material interests and affects
the lives of all the characters in the novel. The legend of Azuera,
evoked throughout the novel, is an explicit rendering of the power
of silver to corrupt and enslave. According to this tradition, "Two
gringos, spectral and alive, are believed to be dwelling to this day
amongst the rocks, under the fatal spell of their success. Their souls
cannot tear themselves away from their bodies mounting guard
over the discovered treasure" (20). The souls of these foreigners
cannot be liberated from their flesh and must remain in the earthly
world until the bodies are freed from the enchantment of the
treasure. The legend suggests the dominance of material (the
body) over moral (the soul) concerns, and the inevitable corruption
of those who pursue the silver.

All the characters in the novel are tested against the silver as if it
were a touchstone of moral worth, and they all wonder, like the young
captain in "The Secret Sharer", "how far I should turn out faithful
to that ideal conception of one's own personality every man sets up
for himself secretly."27 Few are able to remain faithful, for the silver
isolates the characters—isolation is always fatal in Conrad's works—and
destroys love, which like the soul is powerless to redeem the body. The
theme of the novel becomes a synthesis of the lives of all the characters;
for the characters *are* the history, politics and economics, and they
are responsible for the social and cultural changes.

Charles Gould, Nostromo and Decoud are most directly affected
by the silver. The pattern of attraction, enslavement, corruption and
betrayal originated by the senior Gould, is followed both by Charles
Gould and by Nostromo. The elder Gould, who correctly predicted
he would be killed by the mine, begged his son never to return to
Costaguana. Despite these warnings, the fact that his Uncle Henry
had been executed during a bloody revolution, and that a similar
venture (the Atacama nitrate fields) had ended disastrously, Gould
fell under the spell of the mine. Gould believes the mine, which had
been the cause of an absurd moral disaster, must be made a material
and moral success in order to preserve the name and honor of his
family.

Gould's ambitions, summarized in his central declaration early
in the novel (and answered by Dr Monygham much later when it is
apparent that Gould has failed to achieve his aims), are twofold and

in opposition to each other.

> What is wanted here is law, good faith, order, security. Anyone
> can declaim about these things, but I pin my faith to material
> interests.28 Only let the material interests once get a firm footing,
> and they are bound to impose the conditions on which alone they
> can continue to exist. That's how your money-making is justified
> here in the face of lawlessness and disorder. It is justified because
> the security which it demands must be shared with the oppressed
> people. A better justice will come afterwards. That's your ray
> of hope. (80—81)

Unfortunately, the ideals that Gould wants and the country needs
are incompatible with the material interests to which he pins his
faith, and "law, good faith, order, security" are subordinated to the
welfare and success of the mine. Ultimately, money-making is not
justified by security (significantly, it is the security not the wealth,
that is shared with the people), and the oppressed continue to be
oppressed in different ways. A "better justice" never comes, and nothing
is ever bound to come, because the security of the mine is dependent
upon the political stability of the country, and history has repeatedly
proved that permanent stability is impossible to achieve.

The great insecurity of the mine is symbolized by Gould's threat
to blow it up at the time of the Monterist Revolution. The fate of
the mine and all the people connected with it is entirely in the hands
of Gould who would not hesitate to destroy it to protect what he
considers to be his own best interests. The explosives presumably
remain in the mine during the calmer periods that follow the counter-
revolution as a protection against the frequent changes of government.

One of Gould's greatest limitations is that he never fully realizes
the social consequences of his actions. Though exploding the mine
might suit his own interests, it would certainly harm the lives of the
workers and their families under his protection, as well as the economic
and political stability of the entire country. The tremendous power of
"El Rey de Sulaco" is too personal, dynastic and irresponsible. A
second limitation is that Gould never considers what the silver is
used for once it leaves Sulaco; he never fully realizes the potential
evil of the mine and lacks the imaginative estimate of the silver that
his wife possesses. For him, the worth of the mine is beyond doubt.
He has complete faith in the financial empire of Holroyd, who has
mechanized the life of his American employees just as Gould has

done in Costaguana. Holroyd uses his vast profits for further imperialistic ventures and exploitation, and wants to subject the entire world to the inexorable processes that have been transforming, corrupting and destroying Costaguana. When Gould agrees with Holroyd that the mining interests will survive to dominate Costaguana along with the rest of the world, his wife is horrified and calls it the most awful materialism, devoid of the justificative conception or moral principle necessary to sustain it.

Later on, Gould realizes that he too must inevitably be debased by the crime, corruption and intrigue of the country. Like his father, he did not like to be robbed, but in Costaguana he could not work honestly until the thieves were satisfied. The inevitable nature of the mine is to exploit and to be exploited.

Gould's "material interests" speech represents the height of his idealistic ambitions, and reveals that he had dangerously idealized the worth and meaning of the mine. Gould's idealism is uncomfortably close to what Decoud calls "sentimentalism," for Gould is one of those sentimental "people that will never do anything for the sake of their passionate desire, unless it comes to them clothed in the fair robes of an idea" (197). Decoud would agree with Razumov in *Under Western Eyes,* that "Visionaries work everlasting evil on earth,"[29] for he believes that idealism in its insidious form is merely a mask to conceal egoistic ambition.

Dangerously obsessed by his conception of the mine, Gould surrenders his wife's happiness to the seduction of an idea. Emilia Gould realizes that the wealth pouring out of the mine dries up the sources of her husband's sympathy and feeling, and that her life is being robbed both of daily affection and of children. She understands that her mission is to save him from the effects of his overmastering passion, and her failure in this mission is one of the great tragedies of the novel, for she can never make Charles share *her* vision of the mine. "It was as if the inspiration of their early years had left her heart to turn into a wall of silver bricks, erected by the silent work of evil spirits, between her and her husband. He seemed to dwell alone within a circumvallation of precious metal, leaving her outside." (184)

Emilia sees the reflection of her own personal tragedy in the almost imitative pattern of Nostromo's corruption, and the debasement and ruination of his love. In a severe and painfully poignant tone she tells the despairing and mournful Giselle that she too has been loved. When she allows herself to be persuaded by Decoud, decides to withhold the news of the Santa Marta defeat of the Ribierists from her husband, and lets the silver come down the mountain to be sent north for credit, she too becomes involved in corruption. She redeems herself only when she tells the dying capataz, "Let it be lost forever."

Nostromo admires (and is measured against) Viola's idealism in the same way that Charles admires Emilia's; and Teresa Viola's warning of betrayal and destruction echoes that of Gould's father. Though Viola's idealism is admirable, like Emilia's, it is ineffective and even pitiful. Simón Bolívar's statement that those who worked for America's independence have ploughed the sea, is an ironic judgment of Viola's career in South America. The rugged and noble warrior of republican principles who cannot live under a king, subjects his family to exile and far worse tyranny in Costaguana. Yet Viola does have principles of universal love and brotherhood while the early Nostromo thrives solely on adulation, reputation, prestige, vanity and fame. That is the difference between Nostromo, the metaphoric "fellow in a thousand", and old Viola who really was a fellow in Garibaldi's "Thousand".

Nostromo's exploits are legion: he saves Ribiera from the mob, rescues the Viola family, carries Father Corbelan's message to the wild Hernandez, brings Sir John over the mountains, finds a doctor for the dying Teresa, and sails out with the silver of the mine. All these exploits are characterized by a divorce of action from thought. He was called upon, his reputation demanded that he accept the challenge, and he acted — almost instinctively and without reflection.

The extraordinary change in the capataz begins with his possession of the silver, and is signified by his marvelous Adamic awakening and rebirth into a new life at the ruined fort. Nostromo's physical and mental awakening occur simultaneously, initiate his thoughtful phase, and confirm his belief in Teresa's prediction that he has been betrayed by the "hombres finos". Deprived of reputation, Nostromo seeks compensation in wealth, for his prestige was his fortune. The capataz had always lived in splendor and publicity, but awakening in solitude beneath a watchful vulture that symbolizes, and senses in Nostromo, death and corruption, makes him feel destitute: "on a revulsion of subjectiveness [like Gould's egomania], exasperated almost to insanity, [he] beheld all his world without faith and courage. He had been betrayed . . . And Nostromo had made up his mind that the treasure should not be betrayed." (334–335)

Like Gould, he pins his faith to material interests to compensate for a former loss, and this is his undoing, for his life becomes bound up with treasure. Nostromo's stealthy rapacity (contrasted to Sotillo's brazen greed) forces him to abandon Teresa on her deathbed and deny her dying wish; and to abandon Decoud to solitude, silence and suicide. He betrays his love for Giselle (as Gould betrays Emilia), and agrees to marry Linda so that he can continue to "mine" the buried silver on the Great Isabel.

On this island Viola protects his family with an old rifle, just as he did when Ribiera fled, but this time Nostromo returns, not to save Giorgio, but to be slain by him. Viola, who keeps the Great Isabel Light shining upon Nostromo's disgrace, poverty and contempt, slaughters his surrogate and future son, and extinguishes the happiness of both daughters. His mistaken murder is the final sardonic comment on his violent career in South America, where he hoped to die tranquilly among his grandchildren. If Idealism has killed Corruption, it has also killed part of itself, and the victory is pyrrhic.

Decoud, more than any other character, represents the inability of the values of European civilization to survive in Costaguana. He recognizes the conflict between the two worlds and the fatal dualism in the Costaguana character, but cannot reconcile the opposites. "There is a curse of futility upon our character: Don Quixote and Sancho Panza, chivalry and materialism, high-sounding sentiments and a supine morality, violent efforts for an idea and a sullen acquiescence in every form of corruption" (144). The former qualities are the quixotic illusions that Europe brings to Costaguana, the beliefs of Gould, the code of Nostromo, the ambitions of Decoud. The latter ones are the ghastly realities of the country that crush these ideals. The dualism is expressed in the social structure of the country, in the indolence of the upper classes and the mental darkness of the lower, as well as in the deliberately contrasted character types: the fraudulent bravado of General Montero and the offhand fortitude of General Barrios, the ferocity of Bento and the enlightenment of Ribiera, the cowardly brutality of Sotillo and the forthright indignation of Captain Mitchell, the crude demagoguery of Gamacho and Fuentes and the parliamentary principles of Juste López. The dualism is even expressed in the question of Decoud's death, for the general *belief* was that he died accidentally, but the *truth* was that he died from solitude and want of faith in himself and others.

Decoud's idealistic counterpart is Don José Avellanos, an ironic and pathetic figure, who suffers untold horrors under Bento only to die fleeing from the Monterist invasion. His naive and passionate involvement in affairs of state is pitifully misplaced despite the experience of his own *History of Fifty Years of Misrule;* and he represents the death of true nobility that is defeated by greed and rapacity.

In contrast to Don José, Decoud embraces material interests to serve his personal ambitions. He uses the wealth of the mine to bring back a well-armed General Barrios, to effect a Ribierist counter-revolution, and to form a separate and independent Occidental Republic. Though he achieves these ambitions, he betrays his love for the extraordinary and beautiful Antonia Avellanos (a younger version of Emilia Gould), and loses his life.

The testing of Decoud's inner strength and the values of European civilization, of his love for Antonia and his commitment to the Revolution, takes place in the greatest scene of the novel, while the Golfo Placido sleeps profoundly under its black poncho.

> It was a new experience for Decoud, this mysteriousness of the great waters spread out strangely smooth, as if their restlessness had been crushed by the weight of that dense night . . . The solitude could almost be felt. And when the breeze ceased, the blackness seemed to weigh upon Decoud like a stone. . . . Intellectually self-confident, he suffered from being deprived of the only weapon he could use with effect. No intelligence could penetrate the darkness of the Placid Gulf. (214-215, 225)

These dark forebodings are presented as Decoud's first frightening impressions of the gulf while he is still with Nostromo; and only hint at the total disintegration of his personality that is not revealed until much later in the novel.

After ten days of isolation, solitude becomes the state of Decoud's soul, which is no longer protected by his irony and scepticism, his intelligence and passion. He begins to doubt his own individuality, loses faith in the reality of his past and future actions, and beholds the universe as a succession of incomprehensible images. His mental agony is subtly likened to the tortured Hirsch, hanging from a rope that pulls his wrists higher than his wrenched shoulder blades, until Sotillo's pistol shots blast his body and snap his life. Decoud's "solitude appeared like a great void, and the silence of the gulf like a tense, thin *cord* to which he *hung suspended* by both hands . . . He imagined it [the cord] snapping with a report as of a pistol." (397)

In the same way, "the sensation of the snatching *pull, dragging* the lighter away to destruction" that Decoud feels when the boats collide in the gulf, is similar to Linda Viola's brooding jealousy: "A strange, *dragging* pain as if somebody were *pulling* her about brutally" (238, 437). (Italics mine). The effect of these parallel descriptions is to bind all the Europeans in a common moral and physical destruction that can be delayed and transformed, but not obliterated, by idealism or by material interests. Hirsch's torture recalls Monygham's, whose breakdown contrasts to Avellanos' resistance. The execution of Gould's uncle is nearly repeated when Gould is lined up to be shot, just as Monygham is almost hanged by Sotillo—as Hirsch was.

Decoud, overcome by the crushing, paralyzing sense of human littleness as he struggles against the forces of nature in total isolation, shoots himself and uses the silver to sink his body, which fails to trouble the glittering surface of the Placid Gulf. It is Decoud's death and the missing ingots of silver that seal Nostromo to the treasure as the spirits of Azuera possess him forever and make him a lifelong slave.

Dr Monygham's devastating pronouncement to Mrs Gould, which his loyalty and devotion to her force him to make, carries the ideological substance of the novel.   This speech evolves from the history of Costaguana and the San Tomé mine, the terrible effect of "progress" on the traditional life of the people, and the corruption of the Europeans by the silver.   F. R. Leavis writes that Monygham must be counted among the idealists of the novel because the doctor, "for all his sardonic scepticism about human nature, does hold to an ideal. His scepticism is based on self-contempt, for his ideal . . . is one he has offended against; it is an exacting ideal of conduct.   He offers a major contrast with Nostromo . . . [for] his having no reputation except for 'unsoundness' and a shady past, and his being ready to be ill-spoken of and ill-thought of."[30]   Monygham's declaration is an answer, not only to Gould's early "material interests" speech (which even Gould could no longer state with such conviction), but also to the ironic boast of those who, like Captain Mitchell, continue to put their faith in the silver.

There is no peace and no rest in the development of material interests. They have their law, and their justice. But it is founded on expediency, and is inhuman; it is without rectitude, without the continuity and the force that can be found only in a moral

principle. Mrs Gould, the time approaches when all that the
Gould concession stands for shall weigh as heavily upon the
people as the barbarism, cruelty, and misrule of a few years
back . . . It'll weigh as heavily and provoke resentment, bloodshed
and vengeance, because the men have grown different. Do you
think that now the mine would march upon the town to save
their señor administrador? (406—407)

Like Marlow, the people of Costaguana are faced with a choice of
nightmares, a choice of evils, the inevitable result of unprincipled
exploitation and the destruction of traditional culture.[31]

What is wanting in material interests is a moral principle, and in
Nostromo the moral principle is held by the idealists — Emilia Gould,
Giorgio Viola, José Avellanos (and Dr Monygham). When the first
silver ingot was turned out warm from the mold, Emilia laid her
unmercenary hands on it and

by her imaginative estimate of its power she endowed that lump
of metal with a justificative conception, as though it were not
a mere fact, but something far-reaching and impalpable, like
the true expression of an emotion or the emergence of a
principle. (98)

Mrs Gould's pure and almost ritualistic consecration of the silver is a
painful contrast to Nostromo's guilty greed.

The treasure was real. He clung to it with a more tenacious
mental grip. But he hated the feel of the ingots. Sometimes,
after putting away a couple of them in his cabin—the fruit of
a secret night expedition to the Great Isabel—he would look
fixedly at his fingers, as if surprised they had left no stain on
his skin. (416)

The central tragedy of *Nostromo* is the incompatibility of material
interests and "ideas" or moral principles. In Costaguana, as Emilia
Gould realizes, "there was something inherent in the necessities of
successful action which carried with it the moral degradation of the
idea" (414); and Charles Gould's idealization of the silver is his fatal
compromise with the moral principle. The civilizing mission of European
material progress fails in Costaguana because it betrays the "idea",
and corrupts both itself and the entire country. Only *La Chartreuse*

de Parme surpasses *Nostromo* in its ironic and pessimistic portrayal of total corruption.

4

JOYCE CARY:
AUTHORITY AND FREEDOM

Like Conrad, Cary became a writer relatively late in life and had an extensive and exciting career before publishing the first novel at the age of forty-four.[1] He worked with the British Red Cross during the Balkan War of 1912-13 and recorded his experiences in the posthumously published *Memoirs of the Bobotes* (1960). "I wanted the experience of war," Cary says, "I thought there would be no more wars. And I had a certain romantic enthusiasm for the cause of the Montenegrins; in short I was young and eager for any sort of adventure."[2]

His reasons for going to Africa at the end of 1913 had the same mixture of adventurousness and idealism, for he wanted to see a primitive country and was attracted to the constructive political work. Cary was among the six men selected from sixty-four candidates and was sent to Northern Nigeria, the most sought-after area in the Colonial empire. Cary received almost no pre-service training, and writes that "My orders, when I joined the African Colonial Service forty-two years ago, were to develop native institutions and native economy, with the final aim of producing an African state that would govern itself on more or less democratic lines."[3] Cary was a magistrate, road builder, and head of state, and says, "As an acting district officer, in almost the humblest rank of the service, I was in charge of two Emirates, stretching over a region bigger than Wales . . . My orders were to do what I thought necessary and take the consequences if I did wrong."[4]

Cary fought against the Germans in West Africa and was wounded at Mora Mountain, a hill fortress in the North Cameroons that was unsuccessfully stormed twice in the fall of 1915. He returned to the political service after this campaign, and was DO in Borgu, Northern Nigeria until 1920 when he resigned from the service.

A questioning and revaluation of civilization and its effect on primitive life is central to Cary's African novels, which are concerned with the effect of Christianity on traditional pagan religion and the disintegration of African culture after impact with European civilization. Cary often portrays events from a native point of view and explores primitive psychology. In his novels the Africans suffer far more than the whites for they are dominated politically, culturally and socially. Their tragedies occur on three levels and reflect successive stages of cultural assimilation: the primitive bush pagan Aissa,[5] the partially assimilated Mister Johnson, and the Oxford-educated Aladai.

Aissa Saved (1932), Cary's first novel, shows the conflict between Christianity and pagan ju-ju religion, and how Christianity is perverted into ju-ju by uncomprehending converts who are obliged to accept the letter rather than the spirit of Christianity and who regress into absolutism and intolerance. This perversion leads to meaningless child sacrifice that is a parody of the crucifixion. The paradox of evil resulting from good, a reversal of the doctrine of *felix culpa,* suggests that the missionaries have failed, and that Christianity, as it is understood and practised by these Africans, is no better than the brutalities and superstitions of primitive religion.

An American Visitor (1933) portrays the eternal conflict between authority and freedom, a major theme in all of Cary's novels, in an atmosphere of chaos and lawlessness; and the dangers of absolute power. Whereas Bradgate's text is Kipling's "Clear the land of evil, drive the road and bridge the ford",[6] Bewsher shows a deeper understanding of his people and an awareness of their more vital needs, and aims "to preserve and develop the rich kind of local life which is the essence and the only justification of nationalism."[7]

Aissa Saved and *An American Visitor* suffer from a lack of focus and control, a wild proliferation of characters, and a failure to portray any of them in depth or to show their development. Since his characters usually represent attitudes only and have no real life of their own, and his themes are not well-integrated into the dramatic action of the novel, there is little significant artistic synthesis of experience. Cary's third and fourth African novels, however, show a significant improvement, for the lives of the white and the African characters merge into meaningful relationships. Aladai and Johnson, with Forster's Aziz, are the most fully developed and complete portraits of native characters in colonial fiction.

The plot and characters of *The African Witch* and *A Passage to India* are similar. Both novels concern an engaged girl who goes out to the colonies to learn more about her fiancé and to see if she likes official and colonial life. She finds that they no longer share the same values, their love fades and the engagement is broken off. Like Forster, Cary uses club scenes to reveal a cross-section of colonial society, and measures the personality and values of his characters by their racial attitudes. Dryas Honeywood and Adela Quested, Jerry Rackham and Ronny Heaslop, and Aladai and Aziz have much in common.[8] The themes of lack of understanding and the difficulties of friendship between English and natives, the physical deterioration and spiritual corruption of the whites in the tropics, are sounded by Forster and echo through Cary's novels. But *The African Witch* is a far more pessimistic novel than *A Passage to India* because official failures are not redeemed by successful personal relations; and there are no sympathetic and redemptive characters, like Fielding and Mrs Moore, who are able to prevail against the overwhelming cruelty of the whites and maintain civilized standards of behavior.

Aziz and Aladai represent the third stage of cultural development, that of the well-educated and westernized native, who embraces many aspects of western civilization only to be made an outcast and be rejected by white colonial society. Aziz's Indian nationalism and retreat to a Native State after his victory in court are his means of preserving his self-respect. But the Oxford-educated Aladai, in conflict with both the traditional elements of African society led by the Emir, and the pagan elements led by his sister, the priestess Elizabeth, as well as with the whites who reject him, has no viable culture to which he can return, reverts to pagan ju-ju, and ends disastrously.

Mister Johnson is in the intermediate stage of adaptation to western culture, between Aissa's ju-ju and Aladai's Oxford. Semi-literate and half-educated, uprooted from his own culture, he can only imitate but not absorb western culture. He lives with a wife he does not understand and among the pagans whom he both fears and despises, and in an effort to maintain his dignity and set himself apart from the pagans, he worships the vulgar external trappings of western civilization. He seeks to perpetuate the myth "Rudbeck my frien', he loves me too much". But his death is the only event of his fantastic existence that seems to have a reasonable certitude of achievement.

The evolution and development of Cary's characters from the official and aloof Bradgate through Bewsher and Rackham who make attempts, however ineffectual and inadequate, at personal integration with Africans, to Rudbeck, an ordinary person with many faults, who nevertheless becomes involved with Johnson and committed to the moral responsibility that the involvement demands, reflects in miniature the development of Cary as a novelist.

1.   *The African Witch*

The African Witch (1936) begins as the ancient Emir is about to
die and the two principal rivals for his throne gather their factions
and concentrate their power. The most promising Pretender to the
Emirate is Louis Aladai, a nominal Christian, who has been educated
at a mission school, at an English public school and at Oxford. He
has just returned to Rimi from college, without taking his degree, to
press his claim to the throne. Aladai is descended from a princely
line, is high-strung, courageous and idealistic, and is clearly superior
to his rivals in character and intelligence.[9] He wants to give his people
freedom, justice, education and the advantages of European civilization
that he admires so much, for the tentative contact with western life
has been beneficial to Rimi.

Despite the prevailing doctrine of white prestige, some of the
more liberal English like Judy Coote, an Oxford don who knew
Aladai at college and who supports and encourages him in Nigeria,
admire Aladai's qualities. When her fiancé Rackham compares Aladai
to Gandhi, Judy disagrees, and maintains that Aladai wants reasonable
things. "He's most frightfully anxious to do the right thing and to be
appreciated. He's just pathetically ready to take advice, and he really
does know something about the position too. He's been thinking
about it since he was a boy. I know he's got rather romantic ideas —
about the duty of a king and about freedom and education — but he
doesn't use slogans."[10]

Unlike Gandhi, Aladai is not nationalistic and insists on his loyalty
to England. Whereas Gandhi wants to return to the life and values of
the traditional Indian village, Aladai is quite a modern young man and
demands western civilization for Rimi. When Judy answers that Rimi
has a civilization of its own, Aladai tells her, "Rimi civilization! Do
you know what it is? — *ju-ju* . . . You have stopped it — you have
escaped from it — by your English civilization. And then you refuse
it to us, in Rimi."[11] Aladai, who is the only well educated Rimi,
insists that his people have a right to schools.

Aladai maintains that with only a Rimi education he would be like
his people, slaves to ignorance and ju-ju, and that he would be rubbing
his nose in the dirt in front of Elizabeth's house. And this is precisely
what happens to Akande Tom when he is denied education. Discouraged
in his reading lessons, Tom returns to Elizabeth and is bewitched by
her Circean powers as her admirers "watch him change from man to
beast, with a beast's stupid brain . . . he fell suddenly on all fours. He

began to creep along the yard, still muttering. But his arms seemed to grow shorter; his head and blue shirt became lower, flatter, as if they wanted to sink back into the dirt; until he was creeping like a lizard." Elizabeth's adorers "delighted in Tom's misery and terror, not only because he tried to escape from the herd, but because they were sunk in fear themselves; and also because some fragment of spirit in them, which knew freedom and had pride, was enslaved inside them, blind and helpless, and forced to eat humiliation every day." (303)

Tom's ontogenetic retrogression is very close to the anthropoid mentality of Dick Honeywood who hates the country and people, a kind of mentality that is responsible for Tom's bondage to ju-ju. Dick's

will was the servant of nature, the crocodile in the swamp. He had no freedom. He was not a living soul, but a tumour — something pushed up by the blind force of life; as innocent as an imbecile, as a fungus that eats the face of a corpse. (188-189)

Tom, completely enchanted by the terrible demonolatry of Elizabeth (who is officially praised by the Resident Burwash for her moderating control),

lay motionless and soft. His tense muscles had relaxed; his thighs bulged against the earth. As he lay with his head under the blue shirt he seemed to have lost shape; to be spreading like a flattened, boneless mass — a black jelly, protoplasm. (304)

Like Dick Honeywood, his sister Dryas, Rackham, and the "Pagan's man" Sangster, want to keep the country backward, as a kind of museum for anthropologists. Rackham resents the cannibal chief in the Balliol blazer and maintains that "the blacks out here are not fit to run their own show, and it will be a long time before they learn.[12] Meanwhile, we've got to keep the machine running, and the only peaceful way of doing that is to support white prestige."[13]

Rackham and Sangster, who feel threatened by an educated African, prefer the degenerate Salé, Aladai's main rival for the Emirate and the leader of the Moslem faction, who has had little contact with western civilization and has no desire for it, and who promises to carry on in the unscrupulous tradition of the present aged Emir.[14] The Emir's Treasurer, whom the Resident insists must be able to count up to ten, sets the educational standard for the Oriental court that suffers from a lack of honesty and principle, and is in an advanced state of moral corruption and physical decay.

In spite of Aladai's obvious superiority to the Emir and Salé (the young Aladai is favorably compared with the old Emir in three parallel scenes: when on horseback, during an interview with Burwash, and while he is receiving his people), Burwash does not support Aladai's claim to the throne nor does he attempt to turn Salé out of the palace once he is illegally installed there. Burwash, the name of Kipling's town in Sussex, suggests that the Resident is of the old-fashioned Kipling school of colonial administrators. He is above all a bureaucrat and a careerist, and is terrified of having any "unfortunate incidents" in the station. He therefore accedes to the Emir's demand for Aladai's removal from Rimi in order to avoid confusion in the country, disturbance of trade and most important of all, an enquiry from the Governor which would injure his career.

Characteristically, Burwash hides behind a straw hut during the "unfortunate incident" at the races, and is found under a bush with a large lump on his head after the women's riots, which he encourages by hitting one of the women with his car. In a more polished and urbane way, he is as blundering and hopelessly inept as the superannuated Emir. He fiddles with phrasing while Rimi burns, and is a master of procrastination and equivocation who always puts his personal interests before all other considerations. Burwash responds to the suggestions of the Emir and Elizabeth, the two most reactionary leaders in Rimi, but refuses to help not only Aladai, but also the good Doctor Schlemm on three different and urgent occasions.

Burwash is abysmally ignorant of the native language and native life (though he is proud of his ability to understand the psychology of the people), and depends for his information on an African political agent who lies to him constantly. Burwash reports that there are no witch trials while Osi is being burned for witchcraft, and that human sacrifice is unknown while victims are being offered to the sacred crocodile. He is completely unaware of the danger from the rioting crowds, assures Schlemm that there is no cause for alarm, and as the town explodes into chaos and anarchy, he returns to his "real work" in the ant-eaten files. Though his report on the riots is totally inaccurate, he is, ironically enough, strongly commended by the Committee of Enquiry for preventing further bloodshed. He does not understand the cause of the riots,[15] and has learned nothing from them. Early in the novel he tells Aladai of his reactionary bias against education, and he repeats these views to Judy at the end of the book. Yet Rackham praises British rule, represented by Burwash in Rimi, and claims that there is nothing essentially wrong in colonial government.

Fisk, Burwash's reverent assistant, also carries on the Kipling traditions, for his attitude to Burwash is that of a keen young boy to a rugby captain. Fisk wants to bear the white man's burden, and Cary, like Forster, is certain that public school training will not help him to do so. For as Cary writes home from Nigeria in 1917 about the effects of his own public school education at Clifton, "I've been taught to believe, which is really affectation or prudery or snobbery, or prejudice, and which I have allowed to stick in my brain unnoticed till it's dangerous like a fungus, and is beginning to make my brains all mouldy."[16] A remarkable transformation occurs in the obtuse Fisk when Aladai reminds him that he too has been to a public school. Fisk, who has never been able to recognize Aladai as a human being in the context of Africa, becomes quite cordial when he is able to cast the African in the role of a public schoolboy. Unfortunately this sympathy is ephemeral.

Burwash's surprising preference for the ignorant and reactionary Salé over the intelligent and progressive Aladai is explained by the policy of "indirect rule" initiated by Sir Frederick Lugard, who was the first High Commissioner to the newly established Protectorate of Northern Nigeria in 1900 and the first Governor-General of the Colony of Nigeria in 1914. Under the system of indirect rule, Britain recognizes existing African societies and assists them to adapt themselves to the functions of local government. This policy was particularly effective among the dominant Hausa people of Northern Nigeria who have an intense cultural consciousness and show little desire to imitate the white man, and who are therefore far less modern than the more progressive Yorubas and Ibos of the western and eastern regions. Lugard's reasons for establishing indirect, rather than direct rule — extending the British system of law and administration over their African annexations and calling the natives British subjects — were that "The crown colony form of government was manifestly inappropriate for the administration of the vast hinterland regions of the [northern] protectorate... the lack of funds and staff and the existence of strong, well-organized indigenous states (emirates) in that area, convinced him that the emirates should be preserved and used as instruments of colonial rule."[17] Under this system, the younger and better-educated men were often in conflict with the older, illiterate and ultra-conservative tribal leaders.

By supporting the Emir's choice of an illiterate successor, the English reject the western-educated Africans like Aladai who are always the radicals and political reformers, foster the *status quo*, and maintain their control over the ultra-conservative Islamic hierarchy. Cary, like Forster, was prophetic, for only after the Second World War was it officially admitted by the English that indirect rule was "not only a form of government specially invented for backward peoples, but one designed to perpetuate their backwardness by preserving their isolation and tribal [and religious] divisions".18

The sharp conflict between feudalism and enlightenment, ju-ju and education, superstition and civilization, emotion and reason, is expressed in Aladai, as in Kim, by a confusion of identity and a divided personality, and is the central concern of the novel.19 Aladai's tragedy is his defensive retreat from civilization, his reversion to ju-ju and violence when he is totally rejected by the English and must in turn reject them to maintain his dignity and pride. When civilization and civilized values fail in personal relations, education, religion and social welfare, Aladai

> Wandering between two worlds, one dead,
> The other powerless to be born,

is destroyed by the chthonic forces.

Aladai's religion, tastes, ambitions, language, clothes, manners, and possessions are an uneasy mixture of the African and the English ways of life. Though Aladai was Doctor Schlemm's most outstanding pupil at the mission school, he must dissociate himself from the few Christians at Kifi in order to retain the support of the many pagans in Rimi. He has been forced, also for political expediency, to accept the unnatural and uneasy alliance with the followers of Elizabeth's ju-ju and of Coker's heretical primitive-mystic Christianity. He quotes Wordsworth's "Immortality Ode" and appreciates Schubert's *"Ständchen"*, but is even more moved by the poetry and rhythms of the spearman's song in the bush. The "wildness entered into the exhilaration which made him feel that he too, like the boatmen, would like to drink, sing, and dance all night, to perform astonishing feats of rejoicing; and it was also a challenge. It challenged the Englishman in him, who wanted to build, to enrich." (166) When he becomes excited and emotional, he thinks in Rimi, and his English suffers. He has a Bible sewn into his English coat as a successful ju-ju fetish, and wears the coat on top of African dress.   And while fighting in the bush, he furnished his room like an English official's camp.

Judy and Dryas fight for control of Aladai just as they did for Rackham, and each represents one aspect of Aladai's conflict between reason and emotion. Judy, the lame Oxford don, whose physique seems to have suffered at the expense of her brains and nerves, is always thinking, discussing and analyzing. She supports Aladai's educational policy and tries to teach Akande Tom to read, and stands for reason and intellect. Her counterpart Dryas, the public schoolgirl whom Rackham knew "was an ass", plays tennis, performs gymnastics in the symbolically empty education bungalow, and steers the boat while Judy talks. She applauds Rackham's bottle-juggling, is bored by books, dislikes Africa and Aladai, and stands for the physical and emotional qualities. Judy rescues Aladai at the races as Dryas does at the Scotch Club. Judy is involved in riots at the ju-ju house and at Kifi, finds them very exciting, and is twice rescued by Aladai whom she is attracted to and admires; and Dryas dutifully invites Aladai to the Mission and dances with him in the bush. Both women feel guilty about Aladai's estrangement from the English, for when Aladai seeks white society to enhance his prestige, to reach official notice and also to enjoy the company of his intellectual peers, he experiences three painful social rejections, and each one pushes him further from the English, until he is forced to abandon his loyalty to the Crown and his sympathy with English civilization.

The first "awkward incident" takes place at the Rimi races when Aladai and Coker enter the private enclosure reserved for whites and arouse the resentment and anger of people like Mrs Pratt, who demands that the brutes be beaten.[20] Aladai, who was well received by the English in England, naively courts disaster again by appearing without an invitation at the Scotch Club. Just as Aladai's European clothes offended white prestige at the races (where the Emir's representatives were welcomed in their ornamental native dress), so his quotation of Wordsworth is intolerable at the Club, and all the English, led by Rackham, abandon him. Finally, when Aladai returns from the mission with Dryas, Rackham is outraged that he has been alone in the bush with her, and he viciously beats Aladai and knocks him into the Niger. Aladai's emergence from the river, with his European clothes spattered with blood, symbolizes his rebirth as a pagan nationalist and tribal warrior.

The new militant Aladai abandons conciliatory tactics and advocates violence. He tells Judy that riots will attract the attention of the English government who will finally "realize that it is a crime in this country to let a whole nation . . . live and die like their own pie-dogs who starve on every rubbish heap" (265). Aladai's thirst for revenge, blood and power become dangerously like the blood-love and blood-hatred of Coker's religion. Aladai now consciously adopts the role of a human sacrifice, the theme of the song he heard with Dryas in the wilderness:

> She threw herself into the black water
> The river accepted the old woman . . .
> The black water is joyful with her blood, (156—157)

and swears to die for his people.

The fatal force of ju-ju and human sacrifice is also reasserted over Osi, who endures trial, jail, interrogation and torture, until she is freed by Aladai and becomes his adoring companion. Osi embodies a living fear, and her life and death symbolize the tragic power of the ju-ju that has destroyed thousands of intelligent African children. The moment of her sacrifice to the sacred crocodile is the focal point of Aladai's conflict between reason and emotion, between the English and African sides of his personality. His passions moan for blood and country, and his brain, "in a European voice", pleads for peace, trade and schools, until Osi, hobbling pathetically on crippled legs, disappears into the swamp.

Finally, the dark and evil power of the resurrected ju-ju claims its victims in sudden succession: the Emir's Master of the Horse succumbs in anguish to Elizabeth's potent spell; the humane and idealistic Doctor Schlemm is decapitated and martyred by the savage Coker; and when emotion defeats reason, the advocates of emotion—Dryas, Coker and Aladai—are killed. Aladai's death is a bitter comment on the inadequacy of western education and its failure to sustain him outside the sheltered milieu of Oxford, as well as on Aladai's superficial adaptation of western civilization, which cannot withstand the powerful attraction of African ju-ju.

2.   Mister Johnson

Mister Johnson, like *The African Witch*, is concerned with the conflict between western civilization and traditional African society, but the treatment of this theme in the later novel is far more sophisticated and subtle. In *The African Witch* there is a clear dichotomy in Aladai between his superior English characteristics and his inferior African ones, and the effects of western civilization in Rimi are mainly beneficial. In *Mister Johnson*, all of Johnson's most attractive qualities are African while his "English" traits are corrupting and ludicrous; and the effects of civilization, symbolized by the road, are ambiguous. European civilization, which in 1939 appears to be on the verge of destruction, is seriously questioned:

> Bulteel remarks with sudden liveliness, "And how are things at home?"
> [Rudbeck:] "The usual bloody mess."
> "Oh, yes, of course, yes — it's bad." He shakes his head and begins to look serious. "Extraordinary these slumps — nobody seems to have any idea what to do."
> "Looks as if the whole show is going phut."
> "Yes, civilization's in a bad way."[21]

Traditional African life in *The African Witch* consists entirely of violence, ignorance and ju-ju, but the long description of village life in *Mister Johnson* evokes the eternal rhythms of the seasons and the tender familial relations of the tribesmen:

> It is the happy time, the good time of the year when, after months of hard work, a man can live, day and night, in friendship and the joy of his heart. He hunts and his father, uncles, and brothers admire his prowess or sympathize with his misfortunes. At night he squats singing, their voices in his ear, their thighs touching his; he dances with the young men and the young girls spring and wheel before him. He knows them all, he has played with them from their babyhood, they know each other like brothers and sisters; they are like parts of one being. (168)

This is the attractive life that is threatened by the road and will soon disappear.

In Fada, the conservative opposition against the road is very strong. Blore, the DO whom Rudbeck replaces, is deeply conservative, dreads all innovations, and feels that roads corrupt and ruin the unspoiled tribesmen. The Emir and Waziri completely agree with Blore, though for different reasons: they think the road will bring thieves and rascals, and that the road inn will be a refuge for convicts and a fortress against their own authority in the town.

Finally, there is the instinctive conservatism of the pagans, who are most seriously affected by the road and who associate strangers and change with war, disease or "bad magic". To these pagans even Fada station is incomprehensible and terrifying. The road brings the pagan, reluctant and cautious, into the modern age, and those who venture outside their village for the first time are inspired by the music, dancing and beer, and "have already, in five hours, forgotten their dread and contempt of the stranger and their resolve to keep themselves to themselves. In one afternoon they have taken the first essential step out of the world of the tribe into the world of men" (174).

The road brings crime with wealth and prosperity, and forces Rudbeck to question the significance of the "immense canyon" he has forced through the bush:

> Wasn't there confusion enough? Wasn't everybody complaining that the world was getting into such confusion that civilization itself would disappear . . . . We're obviously breaking up the old native tribal organization or it's breaking by itself. The people are bored with it . . . . Are we going to give them any new civilization or simply let them slide downhill? (182—183)

Once created and unleashed, the road seems to have an independent force and energy of its own that changes everything and violently thrusts the old Fada into the revolutionary new world.

It is ironic that Mister Johnson, himself a confused product of the conflict between traditional and progressive life that had taken place earlier in southern Nigeria, should be the inspiration behind the Fada road that abolishes the old ways and transforms the life of the bewildered pagans. One writer of the 1930s calls natives like Johnson "a hoard of quasi-literates, parasitic, litigious, showy, noisy, insolent, and as irresponsible as they are untrustworthy. They wear the white man's clothing, speak pidgin English, and by writing petitions on anonymous charges, can create an activity in Government circles that is as mischievous as it is ridiculous."22   This attitude is very like that of Blore who fears exuberance and dislikes Negro clerks in trousers, who are upstarts and dangerous to the established order of things. Though Blore has no understanding of Johnson, he prophetically warns Rudbeck that the clerk is a dangerous thief.

Though Rudbeck's early evaluation of Johnson is similar to Blore's and Johnson is dismissed by Tring because of these two unfavorable reports, Rudbeck's appreciation and understanding of Johnson develop throughout the novel until he is able to see the clerk as a victim of colonialism. As early as 1909, the administrator Sir John Rodger blamed the English for men like Johnson and wrote in *The African Mail* (Lagos), "We are busy manufacturing black and brown Englishmen — turning them out by the score, and cursing the finished article when the operation is complete.... [We] create an alien and then leave him to work out his own salvation."[23] Kenneth Kaunda, the President of Zambia, expresses the African viewpoint when he states, "The Western way of life has been so powerful that our own social, cultural and political set-up has been raped by the powerful and greedy Western civilization. . . . The result is . . . moral destruction."[24]

But Johnson's moral weaknesses are redeemed by his flamboyant and genuinely creative imagination, his devotion and enterprise, optimism and ambition, courage and resiliency, enthusiasm and invention, amiability and wild exuberance. Johnson feels "too tight with life," "defies the very laws of being," and "is a poet who creates for himself a glorious destiny".[25] Johnson refuses to let dull reality — the ugliness of Fada station, the insignificance of his position, the primitiveness of his wife, or even the danger of his own life — interfere with his imaginative conception of experience. Though he is no longer linked by myth to the world of his ancestors, he becomes a modern myth-maker. He has the fantastic ability to turn his ideal conceptions into reality. He worships, courts and marries Bamu; he invents the road, the means to finance it and the way to finish it. The building of the road becomes a truly creative experience, a village play, a festivity stimulated and inspired by poetry and music.

Johnson's hilarious and erratic filing system, which defies logical connections and soars in fanciful flights, puts native tobacco with elephant poachers because it looks like elephant droppings. After he is severely beaten by the Waziri's men, his description of his victory over them assumes epic proportions and eventually travels across the Sahara to Khartoum and even Mecca. In contrast to Celia Rudbeck, who does not see Africa at all nor the "truth of its real being", Johnson's

> Africa is simply perpetual experience, exciting, amusing, alarming
> or delightful, which he soaks into himself through all his five
> senses at once, and produces again in the form of reflections,
> comments, songs, jokes, all in the pure Johnsonian form. Like a
> horse or a rose tree, he can turn the crudest and simplest form of
> fodder into beauty and power of his own quality. (98)

Since Johnson believes everything he invents, he becomes happier every moment, for he easily convinces himself that Bamu is the most loving wife in Fada and Rudbeck is his best friend.

The ludicrous and pathetic elements of Johnson's character become prominent when he attempts to ape English clothing, manners, and

customs and to force his uncomprehending wife into an alien way of
life. This aspect of his personality is symbolized by his patent leather
shoes and is prefigured by Akande Tom in *The African Witch:* "When
Akande Tom had put on over a naked skin linen coat, trousers, cloth
cap, and black goggles, he felt as near a white man as it was possible for
him to be, and enjoyed an exaltation which might possibly be compared
with that of a risen soul on his first morning in paradise. Because, for
Akande Tom, the change was not only one of appearance, but of being
and power."[26] The slow and deliberate post office clerk Benjamin is a
foil to the impulsive Johnson, and provides an insight into his friend's
character when he says that it is hard for people to go backward once
they have some civilization. For even Gandhi has admitted, "I believed,
at the time of which I am writing [1896], that in order to look
civilized, our dress and manners had as far as possible to approximate
to the European standard."[27]

Johnson wants to transform the beautiful savage Bamu into a great
lady, but his "idea of a civilized marriage, founded on the store
catalogues, their fashion notes, the observation of missionaries at his
mission school, and a few novels approved by the SPCK, is a compound
of romantic sentiment and embroidered underclothes"(8). He is
considered completely mad by his wife, who cannot comprehend him and
who feels she must call the white man to cure his "stranger's illness".
Bamu is more eager to leave Johnson than to follow him; and after the
murder of Gollup, she had her brother betray Johnson to the authorities.
The symbol of Johnson's marriage is the ancient household retainer
Sozy, a "damned idiot" who never understands anything. Johnson's
marriage is an imitation as well as a reflection of Rudbeck's marriage,
for both Bamu and Celia share a rigid and narrow idea of wifely duty,
and neither one of them sympathizes with, understands, or even likes
her husband.

Though Johnson is at the emotional center of the novel, his character
does not develop and his view of Rudbeck remains the same at the end
of his parabolic career as at the beginning. The intellectual focus of the
novel is on Rudbeck, who develops from a passive into an active
character, and finally arrives at a new perception and understanding of
Johnson and of his own responsibility as a colonial official.

Rudbeck, in contrast to Johnson, is totally unimaginative, but like
his clerk, he has a highly mimetic nature. Just as Johnson imitates
Rudbeck, scorns the office routine for "real work" on the road, and
wears a hat exactly like Gollup's, so Rudbeck unconsciously soaks up
the knowledge and even the habits of his seniors. But the inspiration for

all of Rudbeck's most important acts comes from his chief clerk. It is Johnson, sensitive to what interests and pleases Rudbeck, who first proposes the north road that will link with the highway to Kano and attract lorries and traders to the town. Johnson suggests using unexpended votes to finance the road construction during Rudbeck's first tour, and later has the idea of using the *zungo* money to complete the road. And it is Johnson who proposes that Rudbeck execute him personally. Rudbeck's response to Johnson's ideas about construction and finance is enthusiastic, and once the ideas have been given to him, he adopts them as his own and pursues them with his accustomed monomania.

Though Rudbeck, like Johnson, ignores unpleasant things as long as possible, he is familiar with the official routine and is able to make the subtle moral distinctions that are a mystery to the clerk. The impulsive Johnson has no moral discrimination, he merely acts — and suffers. He is the scapegoat and sacrifice, the colonial victim who imitates his masters and is penalized while they escape. Johnson cannot see the difference between appropriating unused funds and writing false vouchers, and making what Rudbeck calls "a real steal". When Tring takes over for Rudbeck, the DO's deficiencies are discovered at the same time as Johnson's. The zealous Tring thinks both men are guilty, but the Resident Bulteel intervenes and Johnson is sacked while Rudbeck is let off with a warning.

Similarly, it is all right when Bulteel adopts Johnson's methods and gives Rudbeck unexpended votes when the DO returns to Fada; but when Johnson, following this practice, collects (or extorts) money from the *zungo* to pay for the laborers, beer and music (and his own expenses), he is fired once again. (In the same way, Johnson is fired by the "savage man", Gollup, for having the same kind of drunken parties as his employer, and for daring to give blows instead of patiently receiving them.) Rudbeck's imaginative growth is revealed when he no longer sees Johnson simply as a thief, but recognizes Johnson's viewpoint and his own complicity in the swindle, and lets him off without a jail sentence.

At the beginning of the novel, Rudbeck is as blind to the reality of Africa and the Africans as Celia. But he later separates himself from Celia's view of the devoted Johnson as "Mr Wog",[28] which Tring calls a real piece of intuition, and thinks of Johnson as an individual human being with whom he has a personal and meaningful relationship. When Rudbeck later admits to Bulteel, "He's the man with the ideas . . . . [he] is still surprised by his own remark. He gazes at Johnson thoughtfully as if *trying to get a new conception of him.*" (162) (Italics mine.)

Rudbeck is forced to clarify his conception of Johnson after the clerk has killed Sergeant Gollup with the frequently flourished cook's knife, because responsibility is concentrated in him as sheriff, magistrate and coroner. Though he wants to protest against the official world at the time of the trial, he uses the mask of impersonal and official formalities—symbolized by his unusual full uniform—to avoid personal responsibility, and he refuses Johnson's last request with the formal reply, "you know, the regulations".

But Rudbeck's eagerness to portray the murder in the most lenient light reveals his truest feelings. His accurate interpretation of the crime as unpremeditated and impulsive is one that had not occurred to Johnson, and suggests his identification and sympathy with the clerk. Though he is forced to find Johnson guilty—the clerk readily confesses, for his only wish is to spare Rudbeck trouble and to justify his own image through a redemption of his master's—Rudbeck recommends a reprieve.

The crucial change in Rudbeck occurs when he judges and blames *himself* and the colonial system that demands the regulations be followed, instead of judging and blaming Johnson. He recounts the three fatal steps in Johnson's decline, and links his fate with that of his adoring clerk:

> Rudbeck sits silent and gloomy. Then he says, "Look here, Johnson,—you remember that advance you asked for? . . . I suppose it wouldn't have made any difference to your little difficulties—getting a few bob in advance . . . .
> That report of mine—I don't know if I was quite fair to you . . . .
> And when I sacked you from the road— . . . you don't think this trouble of yours is partly my fault, perhaps." (245–246)

When Rudbeck finally decides to liberate himself from the regulations by shooting Johnson himself and taking personal and moral responsibility for the fate of the boy who looks on him as both father and mother, Johnson feels relieved and triumphs in the daring inventiveness of Rudbeck, who by this act shares Johnson's creative imagination. The simple and devoted Johnson, who has been betrayed before by Rudbeck, Blore, Gollup, his clerk Ajali, his wife Bamu and her brother Aliu, has ultimately earned the loyalty of "the best man in the world". Rudbeck, with a peculiar feeling of relief and escape from guilt, has discharged his "responsibility according to his own unique conscience . . . . growing ever more *free* in the *inspiration* which seems already *his own idea,*

[he] answers [Celia] obstinately, 'I couldn't let anyone else do it, could I?'" (250) (Italics mine).

Though Rudbeck's execution of Johnson symbolizes the African's tragic role in the failure of colonialism, it also expresses Rudbeck's sympathy and understanding, self-evaluation and personal responsibility, compassion and willingness to share blame and guilt. At that moment Rudbeck makes, like Marlow with the dying African helmsman, "a claim of distant kinship affirmed in a supreme moment", and he illustrates Cary's great humanistic theme: "I am influenced by the solitude of men's minds, but equally by the unity of their fundamental character and feelings, their sympathies which bring them together." [29]

5

GRAHAM GREENE:
THE DECLINE OF
THE COLONIAL NOVEL

GREENE is always exhilarated by moving into an unknown country, and no other part of Africa has cast so deep a spell on him as the mists, swamps and fevers of the West African coast. Inspired perhaps by Conrad and Gide's travels to the Congo, by the African voyages of Rimbaud and Céline, Greene trekked through the Liberian bush in 1934. Conrad wrote apprehensively from Africa in 1890, "After my departure from Boma there may be a long silence. I shall not be able to write until at Léopoldville. It takes twenty days to go there; afoot too! Horrors!"[1] Nearly fifty years later Greene reports, "it was the end, the end of the worst boredom I had ever experienced, the worst fear and the worst exhaustion. . . we had been walking for exactly four weeks and covered about three hundred and fifty miles."[2]

Greene has been to Africa four times. *Journey Without Maps* (1936) records his expedition to Liberia; and *The Heart of the Matter* (1948) was written after his stay in Sierra Leone where he worked on confidential wartime missions for the British government. He reported on the 1953 Mau-Mau rebellion in Kenya for *The Sunday Times;* and in 1959 wrote *In Search of a Character* (1961), the journal of his trip to a Congo leprosarium, the setting of *A Burnt-Out Case* (1961). Greene goes to Africa primarily as a traveller and a novelist looking for material; Kipling, Forster, Conrad and Cary lived in the colonies before they wrote their novels. Thus, Greene's extensive experience in the colonies is different from the personal and professional involvement of the Bombay-born journalist Kipling, the steamboat captain Conrad, the private secretary Forster and the District Officer Cary, and he is something of an outsider compared to them.

A second important difference between Greene and the other novelists is that he writes after the Second World War, which gave the same impetus to nationalism in Africa that the Great War gave to India. The impact of the Great War had altered but not destroyed the imperial idea, and the British Empire survived it. But during the Second World War the Empire was fighting for its very existence, for the serious

defeats in Malaya and Burma demolished the argument that imperial
powers protected their colonies. Clement Attlee announced in 1941,
"We in the Labour Party have always been conscious of the wrongs
done by the white races to the races with darker skins. We have always
demanded that the freedom which we claim for ourselves should be
extended to all men. I look for an ever-increasing measure of self-
government in Africa."[3] This policy was embodied in "The British
Labour Party's Charter of Freedom for Colonial Peoples," and became
a reality when a Labour government was elected in 1945. India became
independent in 1947, and ten years later Ghana became the first
independent African country. Nigeria followed in 1960, and today
there are no English colonies left in Africa.

One of the reasons why *A Burnt-Out Case* marks the decline of the
colonial novel is that by 1961 most colonies had ceased to exist and the
colonial experience had lost its traditional significance. There are no
politics in *The Heart of the Matter;* and in *A Burnt-Out Case* African
politics are completely extrinsic, though not without a strong contemporary interest, for the riots in Léopoldville and Stanleyville, briefly
mentioned in the novel, broke out in 1960 and continued through the
time the novel was published the following year.[4] Dr Colin sardoni-
cally tells Querry that the Africans are dying not of leprosy, but
"of us"; and Greene writes that "Hola Camp, Sharpeville and Algiers
had justified all possible belief in European cruelty".[5] These statements
are true, they are liberal and progressive, but they have nothing to do
with the people in the novel. They are imposed from without, purely
decorative, a comment in passing for the benefit of those who have
read about these African atrocities in the newspapers.

In Greene's novels there is no immediacy of innovation as in Kipling,
no struggle in the novels themselves to create political ideas and attitudes
about subject peoples as in Forster, Conrad and Cary. Greene brings
preconceived social and political opinions to his novels, so that fully
developed native characters and cultural conflicts are absent from his
books. Greene's Africans are neither a forceful and dangerous presence
as in Kipling and Conrad, nor are they intelligent and articulate like
Aziz and Aladai.

The final difference is in Greene's use of setting, for the atmosphere
of his novels, whether they take place in England, Mexico, Sweden,
Indo-China or Africa, is always the same. Greene is obsessed with
failure and seediness, misery and sordidness, humiliation, suffering
and disaster. He limits himself to exploiting the generic qualities
of the various settings to produce his characteristic mood and

effects, rather than approaching the setting on its own terms and utilizing its specific and individual qualities.

What remains in Greene's works is an attenuated form of the colonial novel, with an emphasis on the horrible aspects of the setting and a colonial hero who is characterized mainly (though not entirely) through his relations with Europeans. Religion fills the gap left by the absence of the usual subject matter and provides the characteristic substance of his novels. For Greene, the colonial novel is a well-established genre through which he expresses his private, romantic idea of religion.

Greene's failing imagination and the decline of his creative powers from *The Heart of the Matter* to *A Burnt-Out Case* become clear when the two novels are compared, for the characters of the earlier novel appear under different names and in less substantial forms in the later one. Scobie is now called Querry, the childish schoolgirl Helen Rolt becomes Marie Rycker, Ali is changed into Deo Gratias, the persecutor Wilson is transformed into the manhunter Parkinson, and the pale and tepid orthodoxy of Father Clay reappears in Father Thomas.

The difference between Scobie's journey to Bamba with Ali and Querry's trip to Luc with Deo Gratias indicates the weakness of the later novel. Scobie is deeply and personally involved with Ali, who is almost a part of his family, and the sympathetic *camaraderie* of their old days together is once again established on their journey. But Deo Gratias' function in the novel is to represent a burnt-out case and provide an analogy to Querry's moral leprosy and mutilation of feeling. When Querry attempts to speak to Deo Gratias on this trip, he is unable to do so. Deo Gratias exists purely as a symbol and never comes to life as a human being; we learn nothing about Africans or lepers from him.

Certain characteristic mannerisms and weaknesses of *The Heart of the Matter* become the dominant mode of *A Burnt-Out Case*. Whereas an entry in Scobie's diary leads to Wilson's discovery of Scobie's suicide, Marie's misleading notation in her diary leads to the murder of Querry by her jealous husband. Then the long and intolerably arch adventure story that Scobie invents for the sick little boy is repeated at even greater length in Querry's tedious parable (Querry is "the boy" and God "the king"), which Marie justly criticizes. The sentimentality of Helen's stamp album is also repeated in the grave of Dr Colin's wife and in Deo Gratias' final floral tribute at Querry's grave. And the deliberately ambiguous last words of Scobie, "Dear God I love . . ." are repeated in Querry's last words, "this is absurd or else. . . ." Finally, the inevitable generous priest who says of Scobie, on the last page, the Church "doesn't know what goes on in a single human heart," declares on the penultimate page of *A Burnt-Out Case*, "We don't know enough about Rycker to condemn him."

Certain descriptive passages from the earlier novel are repeated almost word for word in *A Burnt-Out Case*, as if Greene had returned to the first book to salvage what he could use once again. Both Scobie and Querry find their slain or injured servants in the dark of night in precisely the same way. They also live in identical rooms:

> . . . his room: a table, two kitchen chairs, a cupboard, some rusty handcuffs hanging on a nail like an old hat, a filing cabinet: to a stranger it would have appeared a bare uncomfortable room but to Scobie it was home.[6]
> . . . Querry's room. It was the only one in the place completely bare of symbols, bare indeed of almost everything. . . . The room struck the Superior even in the heat of the day as cold and hard, like a grave without a cross. (86–87)

The native medicine bottle, the lizard and moth, the pye-dog, and pink laterite of *The Heart of the Matter* are reproduced in *A Burnt-Out Case*:

> a bottle standing at the corner of a warehouse with palm leaves stuffed in for a cork. . . . Scobie picked the bottle up. It was a dimpled Haig. (34–35)
> By the old deck chair stood a bottle with a Johnny Walker label. It contained a brown liquid and some withered plants. (54)
> The lizard pounced upon the wall, the tiny jaws clamping on a moth. (261)
> The gecko [lizard] on the wall leapt at the moth. (43)
> Why, he wondered, swerving the car to avoid a dead pye-dog, do I love this place so much? (32)
> Querry swerved to avoid a dead piedog. (186)
> The laterite roads . . . became a delicate flowerlike pink. (20)
> the laterite glowed, like a night-blooming flower, in shades of rose and red. (148)

In thirteen years, the brand of Scotch has changed, pye-dog is spelled differently and a few indifferent similes have been added. *A Burnt-Out Case* is an imaginative failure, and like Shakespeare's fire, is "consumed with that which it was nourished by".

Whereas *The African Witch* is influenced by *A Passage to India* and the tradition of the colonial novel, *The Heart of the Matter* is fortified by the voluptuousness of Baudelaire and the austerities of Eliot. In Greene's novel, however, their ideas are not personally assimilated and vitally transformed in a new form, but are rather eclectically knitted together. *A Burnt-Out Case* is not only a weaker version of Greene's earlier novel but also an imitation of Conrad's *Victory*, and it marks the end of the colonial genre.

1.   *The Heart of the Matter*

T.S. Eliot's essay on Baudelaire (1930) announces the theme of *The Heart of the Matter*, for Greene writes in his essay on Henry James: "'It is true to say,' Mr Eliot has written in an essay on Baudelaire, 'that the glory of man is his capacity for salvation; it is also true to say that his glory is his capacity for damnation. The worst that can be said for most of our malefactors, from statesmen to thieves, is that they are not men enough to be damned.'"[7] And in *The Heart of the Matter*, Greene writes, "Only the man of goodwill carries always in his heart this capacity for damnation."[8]   This paradox of the "good man damned" is emphasized in the important eipgraph from Charles Péguy, poet, socialist, republican and Catholic convert, who is the prototype of Henry Scobie: "Le pécheur est au coeur même de chrétienté. . . .Nul n'est aussi competent que le pécheur en matière de chrétienté. Nul, si ce n'est le saint. [Et en principe c'est le même homme]." In *The Lawless Roads* (1939), Greene writes admiringly of Péguy challenging God in the cause of the damned; and at the end of *Brighton Rock* (1938), the old priest tells Rose about Péguy without mentioning his name: "He was a good man, a holy man, and he lived in sin all through his life, because he couldn't bear the idea that any soul could suffer damnation."[9]

Eliot's essay also foreshadows a second religious paradox in *The Heart of the Matter;* the complex identification of damnation and salvation. Eliot states that "damnation itself is an immediate form of salvation—of salvation from the ennui of modern life, because it at last gives some significance to the living";[10] Greene writes of Scobie that "Virtue, the good life, tempted him in the dark like a sin" (203) . Scobie and the whiskey priest in *The Power and the Glory* (1940) are the most extreme examples of Greene's incorrigibly romantic attitude toward sin. From the depths of an infernal Mexican jail, while his fellow prisoners, awaiting execution, copulate amidst the ghastly filth, the whiskey priest is able to remark, "suddenly we discover that our sins have so much beauty."[11]   This important and paradoxical idea derives from the tradition of the sinner turned saint—Buddha, St Augustine, St Ignatius Loyola—and is a variation of Dostoyevsky's belief in redemption through sin.   Although Scobie is no saint, Greene would have us observe his sacred sins with almost divine tolerance: he is a character that Greene admits he "had loved too much".[12]

Greene believes "it was only hell one could picture with a certain intimacy,"[13] and he makes evil perceptible, tangible, odorous, and gives the sinner flesh and blood.   Greene enlarges Scobie's capacity for damnation by confining him to an African hell where the sordid nature of the colonial setting incites his corruption, intensifies his suffering and contributes to his suicide.   The dispirited, fever-soaked Vichy in French West Africa are likened to the rebellious fallen angels on the Heights of Abraham, the English colonists compared to the damned in the Cities of the Plain.   Scobie's definition of hell is "a permanent sense of loss", and he has endured this loss since the death of his daughter.   When he investigates the suicide of Pemberton, whose corpse appeared to Scobie as a sleeping child, he suffers the torments of the damned—*peine forte et dure.*   He can say with Marlowe's Mephistopheles, "this is hell, nor am I out of it", and with Milton's Satan, "which way I fly is Hell; myself am Hell."[14]

In Sierra Leone, the hot, damp and feverish white man's grave on the unfriendly shore of West Africa, the mental anxieties are even worse than the unhealthy air and the blackwater fever; the wounds that fester in the damp, turn green if neglected for an hour and never heal; the physical enervation and diminution of sexual desire.   It is a climate for meanness, malice, snobbery, melancholy, dissatisfaction and disappointment.   Here injustice and cruelty flourish for human nature cannot disguise itself.   The continuous gossip and nervous strain, the isolation and fear of war, the boredom and deprivation, drive young Pemberton to suicide and make Louise cry out against the maddening loneliness.

There is also the ubiquitous presence of repulsive and horrifying creatures—rats and vultures. Disfigured and starving pye-dogs wail and whine or lie swollen and suppurating in the rain-soaked gutters; flying ants sear themselves against stark light bulbs; the splattered insides of crushed cockroaches decorate the walls; mosquitoes breed malaria and dive into proffered gins; and ants are found in fetid meats. The misery is intensified by the tawdriness and dreariness of the standardized surroundings—green black-out curtains, ugly government furniture, hideous rotting cushions—that seem like the furnishings of hell.

Greene's literary conception of hell on earth is derived from Baudelaire and T. S. Eliot. He is strongly influenced by Baudelaire's sordid and profane imagery, atmosphere of despair, insistence on the cruelty of love, sense of the all-pervading evil in the world and belief in the knowledge of sin as a religious experience. Baudelaire's "Spleen: Quand le ciel bas et lourd," for example, is charged with the same atmosphere as Greene's somber and oppressive tropical colony, and with the profound despair of his hero-victim. And Eliot's portrayal of sex as humiliation ("I raised my knees/Supine on the floor of a narrow canoe"), his depressing seediness (the "cheap hotels/And sawdust restaurants"), his insistence on the lack of spiritual values in modern life ("the empty chapel" and "dry bones"), and his rather harsh and joyless religious vision (in *The Four Quartets*), are major themes in Greene's work.[15] The oppressive dreariness of *The Waste Land*—

> you know only
> A heap of broken images, where the sun beats,
> And the dead tree gives no shelter, the cricket no relief,
> And the dry stone no sound of water—

suggest the squalor, corruption and despair in Greene's novel.

Henry Scobie, the squat and grey-haired policeman, seems out of place in hell, for both the Police Commissioner and the unscrupulous Syrian trader Yusef recognize him as a just and honest man. He is sensitive about his wife's unhappiness, understanding and forgiving about his colleagues' frailties, sympathetic to the persecuted Syrians, and wonderfully gentle and compassionate amidst the pervasive intolerance: in Africa he "could love human beings nearly as God loved them, knowing the worst " (32).

Unlike Harris, the ex-public schoolboy who venomously hates the country and the "bloody niggers", Scobie likes the place and admires the beauty of the people. He understands that truth and falsehood, guilt and innocence are relative, and feels an extraordinary affection for the people who paralyze English justice with simple lies. He even feels kindly towards the unctuous and treacherous Yusef.

Scobie's affection for Africans is centered on his loyal, kindly and honest servant, Ali. Scobie has a fatherly concern for Ali who in some ways is a surrogate child, a compensation for his dead daughter, and he associates moments of great happiness with his "boy": "Ali squatting in the body of the van put an arm round his shoulder, holding a mug of

hot tea—somehow he had boiled another kettle in the lurching chassis. . .
He could see in the driver's mirror Ali nodding and beaming. It seemed
to him that this was all he needed of love and friendship. He could be
happy with no more in the world than this." (83—84)

Scobie's suspicion of Ali is the first fatal sign of his growing deceit
and corruption, which he carries inside himself like rotted flesh, for
his faith in the boy had set him apart from the fearful distrust of the
other whites. When Scobie acquiesces to the diabolical plot of Yusef,
who promises to test Ali's fidelity, his damaged rosary, first a symbol
of broken faith and now of broken trust, is given to Yusef's men as a
token. Scobie knows he must ask about Yusef's plan, for the Syrian has
already betrayed him by lying about the jewels hidden in Tallit's parrot
and has blackmailed him with his love-letter to Helen, but he is prevented
by the weariness of his corruption. When he hears Ali's fearful cry and
finds him cruelly slaughtered by the wharf "rats", Scobie condemns
himself: "I've killed you. . . you served me and I did this to you. You
were faithful to me, and I wouldn't trust you," and he confesses to
himself, "I loved him" (277). The evil spirits of the native medicine
bottle, which Scobie disturbed and released on the deserted and
dangerous wharf early in the novel, have had their effect; they were
left to wander blindly and to settle on the innocent, and they have
settled on Ali.

Scobie's tragedy occurs when compassion and love degenerate into a
corrosive and corrupting pity that cruelly destroys love. Torn between
love for his wife Louise and his mistress Helen, by the terrible impotent
feeling of contradictory responsibilities, Scobie asks himself, "Do I, in
my heart of hearts, love either of them, or is it only that this automatic
terrible pity goes out to any human need—and makes it worse?" (227)
His sentimental pity becomes a form of superiority, contempt, egoism
and pride that masks itself as responsibility.

Scobie especially pities and loves failure. He is bound by the pathos
of his wife's unattractiveness, and he wonders if he could have loved
Helen if he had not pitied her first. Helen is aware of his propensity to
pity and angrily rejects it. "But it was not a question of whether she
wanted it—she had it. Pity smouldered like decay at his heart. He would
never rid himself of it. He knew from experience how passion died away
and how love went, but pity always stayed. Nothing ever diminished pity.
The conditions of life nurtured it. There was only one person in the
world who was unpitiable—himself" (192).

But Scobie deceives himself on this point, for he gets as much pity
as he gives. He is pitied by Harris for his wife, by his colleagues for his

failure, and even by Yusef for his integrity, poverty and fatal impotence against adversity. Only toward the end of the novel does Scobie realize that he too is pitied.

Scobie's pity for others and his terribly pessimistic world view are based on both self-pity and on guilt that derive from the death of his daughter. For Scobie escaped witnessing her death while his wife sustained the entire agony, and in the novel he continually pays for the one death he missed. The Portuguese captain's remark that his daughter may save him at last is the "turning-point" of the novel; it convinces Scobie to destroy the illegal letter and sets him on the destructive path of professional delinquency, adultery, sacrilegious communions, complicity in murder and finally suicide. Scobie has no such salvation, and he recognises the truth of his wife's accusation that he has never loved anyone since his daughter died. But he relives the death of Catherine when Ali is murdered and when he watches the death of the shipwrecked girl who seems to wear a white communion veil over her head, just as in his daughter's photograph.

Scobie's guilt is intensified, not relieved, by witnessing the child's death, and he is impelled to sacrifice his own peace to God in exchange for the girl's. Later in the novel, when he learns that Louise is returning from South Africa, he prays for death to avoid causing Louise and Helen unhappiness. And during his profane communion, "he made one last attempt at prayer, 'O God, I offer up my damnation to you. Take it. Use it for them'" (250).

Such bargains with God are very characteristic of Greene and are repeated twice in his later works. In *The End of the Affair* (1951), when the non-believer Sarah Miles thinks that her lover Bendrix has been crushed during a London air raid, she prays, "Let him be alive and I *will* believe. . .I'll give him up forever."[16] The prayer is answered, Bendrix returns unharmed, and she leaves him. Similarly, in *The Potting Shed* (1957), Father William Callifer prays over his hanged nephew James, offering in exchange for his life what he cherishes most dearly: "Take away what I love most . . . . Take away my faith, but let him live."[17] When the boy revives, the priest loses faith.

The interpretation of these bargains with God are at the heart of the novel's matter. Greene told the *Paris Review* interviewers, "I write about situations that are common, universal might be more correct, in which my characters are involved and from which only faith can redeem them, though often the actual manner of the redemption is not immediately clear. They sin, but there is no limit to God's mercy."[18] In a letter to Marcel Moré, Greene comments on Scobie's prayer for the dying child: "obviously one did have in mind that when he offered up his peace for the child it was genuine prayer and had the results that followed. I always believe that such prayers, though obviously a God would not fulfil them to the limit of robbing him of a peace forever, are answered up to a point as a kind of test of a man's sincerity and to see whether in fact the offer was merely based on emotion."[19]

Greene intends us to believe that God accepts Scobie's offer (as He always does in Greene's works) and denies him peace, and that this sacrifice of peace eventually drives him to suicide. The strange effect of this drastic bargain with a God neither just nor lovable, writes Mary McCarthy, is "typical of Graham Greene's peculiar, sensational Catholicism. The truth is that this is the type of bargain ordinarily compacted with the devil . . . a version of the Faustian compact."[20]

Scobie's suicide is motivated as much by his innate Baudelairean pessimism as by his challenging bargain with God. His unhappy marriage to Louise (symbolized by the rusty handcuffs), has taught him the pain inevitable in any human relationship and the difficulty of achieving understanding or happiness. He is convinced it is "an absurd thing . . . to expect happiness in a world so full of misery. . . Point me out the happy man", he declares, "and I will point you out either egotism, selfishness, evil—or else absolute ignorance . . . in human love there is never such a thing as victory: only a few minor tactical successes before the final defeat of death or indifference" (128, 241). Scobie's pessimism inevitably leads to a death-wish. He wants to contract the immeasurably long span of human life so that we sin at age seven and clutch at redemption on a fifteen-year-old death bed.

Pemberton's suicide first plants the idea in Scobie's mind, and at the same time it leads him to self-protecting assurances against suicide. The strictly orthodox Father Clay (whose name suggests more of the earthly than the divine), like Louise after Scobie's suicide, declares that self-destruction puts a man outside mercy; while Scobie, like Father Rank, believes there must be mercy for someone like Pemberton. But Scobie clearly refuses to excuse himself on the grounds of ignorance and insists that he would be damned. Ironically, Scobie protests that as a Catholic he is immune to suicide, for no cause was important enough to condemn himself for eternity.

As the seed of corruption begins to grow (Scobie lives in a swamp and his name suggest scabby and scorbutic), his attitude toward suicide becomes less categorical, and he begins to see purgatorial possibilities. The priests "taught also that God had sometimes broken his own laws, and was it more impossible for him to put out a hand of forgiveness into the suicidal darkness and chaos than to have woken himself in the tomb, behind the stone? Christ had not been murdered: you couldn't murder God: Christ had killed himself: he had hanged himself on the Cross as surely as Pemberton from the picture rail" (206—207).

This characteristic speech reverses the traditional Catholic orthodoxy which, as Father Rank reminds Scobie, teaches one to look after one's own soul, and makes the sacrifice of one's own soul an *imitatio Christi*. Ultimately, Scobie's belief in the mercy of God is greater than his belief in eternal damnation, for Greene has stated that "he wrote *The Heart of the Matter* to show once again the infinite mercy of God."[21] "Against all the teaching of the Church, one has the conviction that love—any kind of love—does deserve a bit of mercy. One will pay, of course, pay terribly, but I don't believe one will pay forever. Perhaps one will be given time before one dies" (231).

Scobie's motives for suicide are to protect the happiness of Louise and Helen and to keep himself from "hurting God". When Scobie takes an overdose of medicine to simulate heart failure, the last words as he "clutched at redemption" are the deliberately ambiguous "Dear God, I love . . ." And Greene's comment on the meaning of these words is equally ambiguous. "My own intention was to make it completely vague as to whether he was expressing his love for the two women or his love for God. My own feeling about this character is that he was uncertain himself and that was why the thing broke off."[22]

Though Scobie had previously told Helen that he loves her more than himself, or his wife, and even more than God, it is clear, from the ending as well as from Greene's statement and from his other works, that Scobie loves both God *and* his fellow men, and that he is not damned. Greene told an interviewer, "I wrote a book about a man who goes to Hell—*Brighton Rock*—another about a man who goes to heaven—*The Power and the Glory*. Now I've simply written one about a man who goes to purgatory."[23] In the final chapter Louise represents the traditional pharisaical orthodoxy that Greene consistently criticizes and rejects, and that he associates with "the plaster statues with the swords in the bleeding hearts: the whisper behind the confessional curtains: the holy coats and the liquefaction of blood: the dark side chapels and the intricate movements, and somewhere behind it all the love of God" (50). (Father Clay, who shares Louise's views, has hideous oleographs and plaster statues in his tiny room.) Louise maintains that her husband was a bad Catholic and must have known that he was damning himself. But Father Rank, speaking for Greene, replies that the Church does not know what goes on in a single human heart, and that Scobie really loved God. Father Rank's explanation is like Scobie's statement to Louise earlier in the novel, that we would forgive most things if we knew the facts, and is essentially the Pascalian maxim, "Tout comprendre, c'est tout pardonner."

This final scene is duplicated exactly in two other works by Greene. In *Brighton Rock* (1938), the old priest tells Rose, Pinkie's widow, "You can't conceive, my child, nor can I or anyone—the. . . appalling . . . strangeness of the mercy of God."[24]   And at the end of *The Living Room* (1953), the inevitable Pharisee and ubiquitous priest discuss Rose Pemberton's suicide. The orthodox Michael Dennis says, your church "teaches she's damned—damned with my wife's sleeping pills", but as always, the unorthodox and more merciful Father James Browne has the last word: "We aren't as stupid as you think us. Nobody claims we can know what she thought at the end. Only God was with her at the end."[25]

The central weakness of *The Heart of the Matter* is that the parallel of Scobie and Péguy is not sustained in the novel. Whereas Péguy, the true religious sinner, could not bear the idea that any soul could suffer damnation, Scobie wilfully exposes Louise to temptation with Wilson, makes Helen commit fornication, and deliberately damns himself. Unlike Péguy, Scobie commits the greater evil to prevent the lesser. Although it is ironic that no positive good comes from Scobie's paradoxically "altruistic suicide"—his deceit is discovered, the insurance is not paid, and it seems likely that Bagster will "bag" Helen and Wilson marry Louise—the irony is wasted because the suicide seems not only without convincing motivation, but even without meaning. Scobie's suicide is theologically, psychologically and humanly wrong, and the religious paradox involved in his merciful fate obscures the necessary distinction between good and evil, while Father Rank's final statement deliberately confuses our understanding of Scobie's act and begs the fundamental moral question of the novel. Greene makes too great a concession to human instinct and says, in effect, that if man has sufficient faith in God's mercy, he can do exactly as he pleases while on earth.

2.   *A Burnt-Out Case:* The Influence of *Victory*

In the Introduction to *In Search of a Character* (1961), which describes the genesis of *A Burnt-Out Case*, Greene confesses that it would probably be his last novel, and in his Preface to *Three Plays* (1961), he emphasizes the extreme strain and depression of composing a novel.

In an interview a year later he repeats, "My last book exhausted me completely . . . . It may be time for me to think about retiring."[26] And in 1964 he confesses in his Preface to *Carving a Statue*, a weak play which failed in London, that it was tormenting to write and fatiguing to produce.[27] Not only does Greene return to *The Heart of the Matter* to compensate for his lack of inspiration and imaginative exhaustion, but he is also forced to succumb to the potent spell of his former master, Joseph Conrad.

Greene mentions Conrad as an unconscious influence in his *Paris Review* interview and admits that his first three novels were influenced by Stevenson and Conrad. He writes that *"Heart of Darkness* impressed Africa as an imaginative symbol on the European mind",[28] and mentions Conrad five times in the first thirty-seven pages of *In Search of a Character.*

Greene quotes from *Heart of Darkness* twice, and states that the river has not changed since Conrad's day. He notices how often Conrad compares the concrete to the abstract, and asks if he has caught the trick. Conrad and *Heart of Darkness* are mentioned in Greene's novel by the journalist Parkinson to add a literary allusion to his description of local color. Conrad's Inner Station and the leprosarium both mark the furthest limit of human penetration. Most important of all, Greene writes: "Reading Conrad—the volume called *Youth* for the sake of *Heart of Darkness*—the first time since I abandoned him about 1932 because his influence on me was too great and too disastrous. The heavy hypnotic style falls around me again, and I am aware of the poverty of my own. Perhaps now I have lived long enough with my poverty to be safe from corruption. One day I will again read *Victory*."[29] But Greene is not quite safe from Conrad's influence, for the tin-pot steamboat, the oppressive jungle, and the symbolic significance of the Congo are very like *Heart of Darkness.*

Though *Heart of Darkness* was in Greene's thoughts when he was writing *A Burnt-Out Case*, it is Conrad's *Victory*, which Greene has called one of the "great English novels of the last fifty years,"[30] that exerts the most powerful influence on Greene's novel. The influence of *Victory* on *A Burnt-Out Case* provides a classic example of how a lesser writer turns to a greater one when his creative resources fail.[31]

Greene follows Conrad's ironic plot rather precisely, for both novels concern the flight to a remote tropical retreat by a lonely man who attempts to extinguish all human emotions. Both heroes are non-believers who on two related occasions become unwilling subjects of a legend. They are both victims of an unsought love that forces them, against their principles, to become involved in the lives of others. As the outside world breaks into their isolation half-way through the novel, they meet their death and achieve their victory or cure.

Querry's personality and beliefs are like Heyst's in several important ways and undergo a similar transformation in the course of the novel. Their names suggest the kind of men they are: *nomina sunt numina.* Axel (excel) and Heyst (highest) indicate a certain nobility of character, just as Querry connotes query, quarry, queer, quest and weary as well as wherry and ferry, his modes of transport on the river. Heyst is a Swedish baron; and Rycker (wrecker) repeatedly refers to *the* Querry as though it were a title of nobility and wonders why the Catholic Church has not made Querry a count of the Holy Roman Empire.

Both Heyst and Querry are reflective and have a taste for solitude that is expressed in their remote and isolated habitations: Heyst is enchanted with islands, and Querry is happy at the leprosarium. Querry's human involvement and emotional awakening are also a precise imitation of Heyst's. There is a direct connection between Heyst's relation to Morrison and Lena-Alma, just as there is between Querry's relation to Deo Gratias and Marie Rycker.

Heyst is a more profound and convincing character than Querry because we are shown his inner life and watch his real self emerge in the course of the novel through his involvement with Lena. Querry's past life and spiritual degeneration are revealed by means of a rather obvious parable, and his character is often presented by a rather facile interpretation of dreams. Since he has only an accidental and cursory relationship with Marie, his transformation in the novel is somewhat unconvincing.

The involvement of Heyst and Querry with Lena and Marie leads to the intrusion of the hostile outside world upon their solitude, and the pursuit, persecution and destruction of the men. It is significant and ironic that both men assist in their own destruction by helping their enemies when they are weakest. Heyst pulls the withered Jones on to the jetty, and Querry carries the feverish Parkinson to the leprosarium. The manhunt illustrates the central irony of the novels, the affirmation of Heyst (and Querry) that he is in no one's way and that nothing could break into his life. They are killed just as they begin to find a meaning in life and a reason for living, and they pay for their former sins against humanity—their evasion of social responsibility and love— after they have reformed.

The themes of the two books are also similar. In both novels the men have an unusual sympathy and pity for a woman that makes them feel human again. Heyst has a new ardor to live and abandons his cherished negations. After telling Marie the story of his life, Querry has an odd elation of human feeling, and for the first time in years seeks human companionship with the mission boat captain. Both novels stress the nourishing power of love, and would agree with Dostoyevsky that Hell "is the suffering of being unable to love".[32] Love gives the characters strength and a growing awareness of themselves and the world, just as hatred weakens Schomberg and blinds him to realities about himself, his wife and other men.

As Lena achieves "her tremendous victory, capturing the very sting of death in the service of love", Heyst realizes "woe to the man whose heart has not learned while young to hope, to love—and to put its trust in life."[33]   Conrad's theme of Christian love is revealed when Heyst regains his soul by rescuing Alma, whose name means soul. In showing her victory through self-sacrifice and death, Conrad emphasizes the importance of the inner or spiritual life as opposed to the external or physical one. In his deliberately exaggerated portrayal of Jones, Ricardo and Pedro, Conrad shows the presence and power of evil in the world and how easily good men can be overcome by potent cruelty.

The theme of *A Burnt-Out Case* is constructed on the analogy between Querry and Deo Gratias. As Greene writes: "Leprosy cases whose disease has been arrested and cured only after the loss of fingers or toes are known as burnt-out cases. This is the parallel I have been seeking between my character X and the lepers. Psychologically and morally he has been burnt-out. Is it at that point that the cure is effected?"[34] It is. Querry has been so ravished by his own false belief and false "love" affairs that he can be corrupted no more. The comparison with Deo Gratias means that this corruption is actually a process ordained by God that leads to Grace through Christian love. When Querry could no longer love, the motives for work failed him, and he experienced the crisis that drove him to the Congo. But Querry has been cured of his former sin, and tells Parkinson, "you can't believe in a god without loving a human being or love a human being without believing in God" (138).

A Burnt-Out Case is so strongly influenced by and heavily indebted to *Victory* that is virtually a diluted and derivative version of the greater novel. After thirty years Greene is still not "safe from corruption" by Conrad whose influence is "too great and too disastrous," for Greene's search for a character led him not only to the heart of darkness, but to Conrad's Axel Heyst.

3.   A Burnt-Out Case: *Setting, Theme and Language*

Querry's reasons for coming to the Congo are the same as those expressed by Greene in *Journey Without Maps* (1936). For Querry, the Congo is a retreat, an escape from the world, a place to find peace, a means to find himself, "a region of the mind". "When one sees to what unhappiness, to what peril of extinction centuries of cerebration have brought us," writes Greene, "one sometimes has the curiosity to discover if one can from what we have come, to recall at what point we went astray."[35] Greene discovered childhood associations at a masked dance in Liberia, and African songs evoke ancestral voices and memories in Querry. Like Greene, Querry finds the deeper and purer sense of terror in the jungle a welcome distraction from the emptiness of modern life, and he admires the bareness, simplicity and instinctive friendliness of the primitive people.

Greene also writes that the fascination of Africa is "a religious fascination: the country offers the European an opportunity of living continuously in the presence of the supernatural. The secret societies, as it were, sacramentalise the whole of life."[36] In *A Burnt-Out Case*, Greene associates African and biblical lepers to produce his version of the leper as saint and leprosy as the way to the holy life. When Dr Colin remarks that people learn their strange ideas about leprosy from the Bible, he is thinking of passages like Leviticus xiii. 45–46: "And the leper in whom the plague is, his clothes shall be rent, and his head bare, and he shall put a covering upon his upper lip, and shall cry, unclean, unclean. All the days wherein the plague shall be in him he shall be defiled; he is unclean: he shall dwell alone; without the camp shall his habitation be." The stigma of the leprous untouchables signifies their "grace of affliction," for the incurable old African leper who inquired after the doctor's health as though it were the doctor who was sick is attractive, sympathetic and brave.

Those who dwell with the lepers and invite them to share a habitation *within* the camp participate in the leper's saintly passion. Dr Colin states the theme of the novel when he says that "the search for suffering and the remembrance of suffering are the only means we have to put ourselves in touch with the whole human condition. With suffering we become part of the Christian myth" (151). Dr Colin's pronouncement to Deo Gratias, who had lost all his toes and fingers, "You are cured," and especially his courageous hope for the afflicted little boy of a gradual cure with no mutilations, are an *imitatio Christi:* "And behold, there came a leper and worshipped him, saying, Lord, if thou wilt, thou canst make me clean. And Jesus put forth his hand, and touched him, saying, I will; be thou clean. And immediately his leprosy was cleansed" (Matthew viii. 2—3).

Querry's moral regeneration in the novel is measured by his pity and sympathy for human suffering. He moves from a feeling of discomfort, to a desire to suffer, to suffering itself. Querry is a "hollow man" and is described by the epigraph from Dante, "Io non mori, e non rimasi vivo." At the beginning of the novel Querry is the antithesis of the moral and attractive Scobie. Querry wants nothing; Scobie wants promotion and money and Helen. Querry no longer knows what suffering is; Scobie suffers intensely. Querry has lost faith; Scobie has fervent belief. Querry has lost the capacity to love; Scobie loves Louise, Helen and Ali. Querry feels no pity; Scobie is suffused with pity.

Querry's sympathetic involvement with Deo Gratias and Marie, his curiosity about people, his desire for companionship and his ability to laugh mark his moral reawakening. In the tropical leprosarium, even Querry learns self-sacrifice and reintegrates himself into the human community. Though Querry had been the "most miserable sinner" "joy shall be in heaven over one sinner that repenteth, more than over ninety and nine just persons, which need no repentance" (Luke xv. 7).

The religious theme of A Burnt-Out Case, like that of The Heart of the Matter, is revealed in the Greenean antithesis between the hollow phrases and thwarted instincts of the priests and pious people, the pharisaical faux dévots; and the crypto-Christians and intelligent men who make their lives without a God. But in his attempt, as Greene says, "to give dramatic expression to various types of belief, half-belief, and non-belief" (vii) in the persons of the Father Superior, Rycker and Father Thomas, Querry and Dr Colin, he fails to embody his theme in living characters, to make the abstract perceptible, tangible and vivid. His novel is too theoretical and too impersonal.

Greene's intention is to lead us to the altar through the church crypt rather than through the front portal, and his references to conventional Catholicism are entirely negative. The Bishop is a cavalier and worldly, the Mass "a whisper, a tinkle, a jingle, a shuffle" (95), the sermon banal and meaningless, and extreme unction "some mumbo-jumbo." Greene's favorite device is the degrading religious simile: refectories are like colonial airports, a Saint Christopher medal like a fetish, the Pope like an eccentric headmaster, Mass like the smell of a medicine, and Christ like an amoeba.

Greene also reverses this technique, loads the novels with religion for spiritual and intellectual ballast, and gratuitously introduces words with churchly connotations to awaken in the reader religious sentiments that have no justification in the action of the novel. Thus, Parkinson sounded like Saint Paul, a cardboard box is carried elevated like a monstrance, and leprophils "would rather wash the feet with their hair like the woman in the Gospel than clean them with something more antiseptic" (19).

This last simile indicates another serious weakness in the book, the imperfect use of language and "poverty of style" that is especially noticeable in Greene's similes, and that indicates the enervated quality of the novel. The act of the woman in the Gospel (Luke vii. 38–50) is *caritas*, that of the leprophil is morbid masochism. In Greene's similes there are "heterogeneous ideas yoked by violence together," *without* the surprising recognition of witty similarity, and too many similes are distracting, awkward or inappropriate.[37]

There is also an over-insistence on simile in the novel that is a certain sign of Greene's lack of sureness in prose and failure of imagination. This is particularly evident in the morbid description of Deo Gratias' mutilated members. Within two pages, Greene writes that he has "hands, like boxing gloves," an "arm like a hammer," knuckles "like a rock" and a fist "like a paper weight" (65–67).[38]

When similar passages from Conrad and Greene are compared, the difference between the vital and dynamic prose style of a living tradition and the debilitated style of an attenuated form becomes obvious.

> on we went again into the silence, along empty reaches, round the still bends, between the high walls of our winding way, reverberating in hollow claps the ponderous beat of the stern wheel. Trees, trees, millions of trees, massive, immense, running up high; and at their foot, hugging the bank against the stream, crept the little begrimed steamboat, like a sluggish beetle crawling on a floor of a lofty portico. It made you feel very small, very lost.[39]

> . . . sometimes he simply watched the steady khaki flow of the stream, which carried little islands of grass and water-jacinth endlessly down at the pace of crawling taxis, out of the heart of Africa, towards the far-off sea.
>   On the other shore the great trees, with roots above the ground like the ribs of a half-built ship, stood out over the green jungle wall, brown at the top like stale cauliflowers. The cold grey trunks, unbroken by branches, curved a little this way and a little that, giving them a kind of reptilian life. (27)

Conrad's rhythmic description shows the psychological effect of the relation of man, the "sluggish beetle," to "massive immense" nature. Greene's flat description has two common-place similes in one sentence, two banal clichés ("heart of Africa" and "far-off sea") and describes man and then nature without showing their integral relationship.

The wooden and abstract characters, the weak and unconvincing theme, and the undistinguished style of *A Burnt-Out Case,* an inferior imitation of *The Heart of the Matter* and *Heart of Darkness* as well as *Victory,* and a novel that marks the decline of Greene's creative powers, brings the important tradition of the colonial novel to an end.

CONCLUSION

The informed and sympathetic novelist who writes of settings outside his own country can use his objectivity and insight to make a valuable contribution to the native tradition, as did Stendhal, James, Mann, Lawrence and Malraux. It is precisely these contributions that are also made by Kipling, Forster, Conrad, Cary and Greene. In the case of Africa, however, where there was virtually no native tradition of literature, the colonial novelists have provided the subject of cultural conflict, and a traditional novelistic form and genre that has inspired the African novel in English. The phoenix of the African novel has risen from the ashes of the colonial novel, for with independence has come a cultural and intellectual liberation, and an articulate literary tradition that re-interprets the European view of African history and civilization.

Chinua Achebe, who is the best of the new generation of West Africans writing in English and who has produced one very good novel and three interesting ones, has commented on the influence of Cary's *Mister Johnson* on his works. "Perhaps he helped to inspire me, but not in the usual way. I was very angry with his book *Mister Johnson*, which was set in Nigeria. I happened to read this, I think, in my second year (at the University) and I said to myself: 'This is absurd. . . . If anybody without any inside knowledge of the people he's trying to describe can get away with it, perhaps I ought to try my hand at it.'[1]

Achebe writes in the final stage of colonialism—the period of independence, and he concludes the story of imperialism that reached its apogee when Kipling began to write. Achebe's books begin with the coming of the white man to the bush and end in contemporary Lagos, and show the process of cultural and moral disintegration that results from colonialism. When asked about the moral view of his first novel, *Things Fall Apart* (1958), Achebe replied: "I feel that this particular society had its good side—the poetry of the life; the simplicity, if you like; the communal way of sharing in happiness and in sorrow and in work and all that. It also had art and music. But it had this cruel side to it and it is this that I think helped to bring down my hero."[2] This hero, Okonkwo, "saw himself and his fathers crowding round their ancestral shrine waiting in vain for worship and sacrifice and finding nothing but ashes of bygone days, and his children the while praying to the white man's god."[3] Achebe's novels reveal the changing perspectives of each succeeding generation, which have also been described by the Nigerian leader, Awolowo, before independence: "Our grandfathers with unbounded gratitude adored the British. . . . Our immediate fathers simply toed the line. We of today are critical, unappreciative, and do not feel that we owe any debt of gratitude to the British. The younger elements in our group are extremely cynical, and cannot understand why Britain is in Nigeria."[4]

Arrow of God (1964), more ambitious than Achebe's earlier novels, was written to demonstrate the existence, the beauty and the value of the African culture that was destroyed by the coming of the whites. The chief priest laments, "there is no escape from the white man . . . . As daylight chases away darkness so will the white man drive away all our customs. . . . What could it point to but the collapse and ruin of all things? Then a god, finding himself powerless, might take to his heels."[5] This novel also opposes the white view of African history as savagery, chaos and stagnation that has been prevalent since the zenith of imperialism, and has provided the necessary justification for conquest

prominent men as Sir Alan Burns, who asserts of precolonial Nigeria:

> Free men also suffered from the cruelty and rapacity of indigenous rulers. They were liable, at the whim of a chief or through the instigation of a fetish-priest, to indescribable tortures and brutal punishments. Trade was hampered by bad communications and the depredations of robbers and pirates who plundered and murdered peaceful traders. Tribal warfare caused much loss of life and destruction of property.[7]

The corollary of this historical misconception is Burns' traditional "defense of colonies":

> We have developed backward countries by the construction of roads and railways, we have opened up mines and improved on the primitive agriculture of the past. We have allowed trade to develop under the protection of a firm administration.[8]

But the colonial novelists deny the validity of this purely materialistic argument and, more importantly, criticize the human degradation of colonialism. Greene believes that:

Civilization in West Africa remains exploitation; we have hardly improved the natives' lot at all, they are as worn out with fever as before the white man came, we have introduced new diseases and weakened their resistance to the old, they still drink from polluted water and suffer from the same worms, they are still at the mercy of their chiefs.[9]

The most striking feature of colonial novels is that the colonial experience is consistently portrayed in a negative light. *A Passage to India* ends with an emphatic negation that is also expressed in the central symbol of the caves—the paralyzing force of shape without form, experience without meaning. The painful deaths of Hummil and Ameera, the rapine and violence of Peachey and Dan, and the self-betrayal of Kim; the horrors of the grove of death, the depravity of Kurtz, and the corruption of Nostromo, Gould and with them all of Costaguana; the slaughter of Aladai and execution of Johnson; the suicide of Scobie and murder of Querry, all these express the terrible failure of colonialism in emotional, moral and spiritual terms.

The colonial novelists insist that a European "civilization" responsible for barbarous wars and inhuman oppression cannot accuse Africans of cruelty and must not strive to impose their standards upon other cultures. Their heroes are both witness and judge of colonialism, and evaluate the colonial experience from a spiritual and moral rather than an economic and political perspective. Their cultural relativism suggests an ample moral vision and teaches the extent and value of human variety, and the emotions of understanding and forgiveness. Their novels illuminate our lives, for they are directly related to contemporary events and problems. They deal with nationalism, the strongest human force of the twentieth century, and provide valuable insights into the conflicts that still exist in India and Africa.

NOTES

Introduction

1 These novels include Haggard's *King Solomon's Mines* (1885), Henty's *Through the Sikh War* (1893), Mason's *The Four Feathers* (1902), Maugham's *The Explorer* (1907), Buchan's *Prester John* (1910), Wren's *Beau Geste* (1924) and Forester's *The African Queen* (1935).

2 These novels include Orwell's *Burmese Days* (1934), Dinesen's *Out of Africa* (1937), Elspeth Huxley's *Red Strangers* (1939), Paton's *Cry the Beloved Country* (1948), Lessing's *The Grass is Singing* (1950), Gordimer's *A World of Strangers* (1958) and Burgess' *The Long Day Wanes: A Malayan Trilogy* (1956—59).

3 Compare Rider Haggard, *King Solomon's Mines* (New York: Collier 1962), 79: "being a Hottentot, the sun had no particular effect" on him, with Graham Greene, *In Search of a Character* (New York 1961), 12: "It is strange how even the African is not acclimatized to this humidity and heat."

4 Rudyard Kipling, "Letters of Marque", *From Sea to Sea,* (London 1919) I 125.

5 Wilfred Stone, *The Cave and the Mountain: A Study of E.M. Forster* (Stanford 1965), 310.

6 Joseph Conrad, "Heart of Darkness," *Three Great Tales* (New York 1960), 256.

7 Joyce Cary, "Preface" to *The African Witch* (New York 1963), 310.

8 Graham Greene, *Journey Without Maps* (New York 1961), 308, 193. Rimbaud, Céline, and Gide also felt the primeval attraction of Africa.

9 Only Kipling maintains a positive attitude toward technology.

10 D.H.Lawrence, *Aaron's Rod* (New York: Compass 1965), 281: "I would very much like to try life in another continent, among another race. I feel Europe becoming like a cage to me. Europe may be all right in herself. But I find myself chafing. Another year I shall get out. I shall leave Europe. I begin to feel caged."

11 ˙Joseph Conrad, *Nostromo* (New York: Signet 1960), 89. Forster expresses the same view in *Howards End* (New York: Vintage 1959), 323: "The imperialist is not what he thinks or seems. He is a destroyer. He prepares the way for cosmopolitanism, and though his ambitions may be fulfilled, the earth that he inherits will be grey."

12 E. M. Forster, *The Hill of Devi* (New York 1953), 8.

13 Graham Greene, *"Abyssinia"* (1935), *Garbo and the Night Watchman*, ed. Alastair Cooke (London 1937), 208.

14 Joyce Cary, *An American Visitor* (New York: Anchor 1963), 260.

I Rudyard Kipling

1W. H. Auden, "The Poet of the Encirclement", *Literary Opinion in America*, (ed. Morton Zabel) (New York: Harper 1962). I 260.

2Joseph Conrad, "Outpost of Progress", *Tales of Heroes and History* (New York: Anchor 1960) 251.

3The narrator believes they will be cut up the minute they reach Afghanistan; the horse-dealer in the Serai predicts Dan will either be raised to honor or have his head cut off, and both things happen. The narrator again warns they would find certain and awful death; and Dan tells his people "I'll make a damned fine Nation of you, or I'll die in the making."

4Charles Carrington, *Rudyard Kipling: His Life and Work* (New York 1955) 81: "Socially, the private soldiers were in fact drawn from the unemployed or unemployable, so that 'going for a soldier' was, in the respectable working-class, regarded as the last degradation, analogous with 'going to the bad.' "

5Peachey and Dan claim they are "going up to Kabul to sell toys to the Amir."

6Philip Woodruff, *The Men Who Ruled India* (London 1965) II 140.

7For a similar view of Brooke see Sir Steven Runciman, *The White Rajahs* (Cambridge 1960) 156: "If there is any meaning in the word greatness, James Brooke was a great man."

8Compare this with Rudyard Kipling, "Letters of Marque", *From Sea to Sea*, (London 1919) I 195–196:
There are States where things are done, and done without protest, that would make the hair of the educated native stand on end with horror . . . . A year spent among native States ought to send a man back to the Decencies and the Law Courts and the Rights of the Subject with a supreme contempt for those who rave about the oppressions of our brutal bureaucracy.

See also Forster's sympathetic portrayal of a Native State in *The Hill of Devi* (1953).

[9]Compare this with Kipling, *From Sea to Sea* I 21, on the empty palace at Amber: "The wise man will visit it when time and occasion serve, and will then, in some small measure, understand what must have been the riotous, sumptuous, murderous life to which our Governors and Lieutenant-Governors, Commissioners and Deputy Commissioners, Colonels and Captains and the Subalterns, have put an end."

[10]For a sympathetic view of these tribesmen, see the early anthropological studies by Kipling's contemporaries: Major J. Biddulph, *Tribes of the Hindu Kush* (Calcutta 1880), and George Robertson, *The Kafirs of the Hindu Kush* (London 1896).

[11]For a similar historical incident see Arnold Fletcher, *Afghanistan: Highway of Conquest* (Ithaca, N.Y. 1965) 148: "four Afghan armies were secretly concentrated . . . on the borders of Kafiristan. In the winter of 1896 these columns converged, catching the Kafirs by surprise and winning an easy victory in a matter of forty days. The triumph is rendered less splendid, however, by the fact that most of the Kafirs were still armed with bows." These brutal tactics were often used against colonial peoples with traditional weapons, from the Mahdi's charge at Omdurman to the Abyssinian campaign.

[12]Kipling, "For All We Have And Are."

[13]Edmund Burke, "Speech on Mr. Fox's East India Bill," *Works,* (Boston 1869), II,462.

[14]Joseph Conrad, *Victory* (New York 1924), 167.

[15]John Hobson, *Imperialism* (London, 1902), 242—243.

[16]The strong influence on Kipling of Twain, whom Kipling met in America and called "a revered writer . . . [whose] keen insight into the soul of men . . . I had learned to love and admire fourteen thousand miles away" (*From Sea to Sea,* II 186, 193), has rarely been noted and never sufficiently emphasized. (Cf. Henry Varley, "A Study in the Career of Rudyard Kipling," *Summaries of Doctoral Dissertations, University of Wisconsin* XIV (1953) 453: "The only clearly evident influence on Kipling's writing is Bret Harte.") Twain's fake Duke and Dauphin, his use of vernacular dialect, his mixture of sentimentality and sadism, his lowbrow philistinism, his heavy-handed use of farce and taste for practical jokes, and especially his admiration for ingenuity and resourcefulness, his respect for expertise and excellence in work, his use of technical description, and his reverence for men who are "honest, trustworthy, faithful to promises and duty" (*Life on the Mississippi,* ch. 3), are all reflected throughout Kipling's work. A fundamental

weakness of both writers is that they never became completely mature. (See Forster's review of Kipling, "The Boy Who Never Grew Up", *The Daily Herald,* London, 9 June 1920, 7.)

[17]Cleanth Brooks and Robert Penn Warren, *The Scope of Fiction* (New York 1960) 29–30.

[18]The slaughter of the camels and then the mules en route to Kafiristan foreshadows the slaughter of the natives. Even the name Carnehan suggests carnage.

[19]Paul Fussell, Jr., "Irony, Freemasonry and Humane Ethics in Kipling's 'The Man Who Would be King' " *ELH* XXV (1958) 231.

[20]Quoted in Carl Bodelsen, *Studies in Mid-Victorian Imperialism* (London 1960) 28.

[21]The identification of Dravot with Prometheus, "his body caught on a rock," like that of Mulvaney at the end of "The Courting of Dinah Shadd," forces a mythical significance on the characters that is not justified in the story.

[22]Fussell, 227.

[23]Brooks and Warren, 151.

[24]Fussell, 219 (italics mine). But before his sacrifice Dan ignobly and unjustly blames Peachey for their downfall: "'It's your fault,' says he, 'for not looking after your Army better. There was a mutiny in the midst and you didn't know.' "

[25]See Carrington, 208, quoting a letter by Kipling written in 1897: "We're about the only power with a glimmer of civilization in us. I've been round with the Channel Fleet for a fortnight and any other breed of white man, with such a weapon to their hand, would have been exploiting the round Earth in their own interests long ago."

[26]The narrator speaks for Kipling when he says of Afghanistan, "no Englishman has been through it. The people are utter brutes," and also when he disagrees with the "politics of loaferdom". He tries to discourage Peachey and Dan from going to Kafiristan, not on moral grounds, but because of the great danger involved. For the most part, the narrator is morally neutral and outside the action of the story. His main function is to lend a sober reliability to the otherwise fantastic tale.

[27]Elliot Gilbert, " 'Without Benefit of Clergy': A Farewell to Ritual," *Kipling and the Critics* (ed. Elliot Gilbert) (New York: Gotham 1965) 181.

[28]A variation of this pattern is found in "Georgie Porgie" (*Life's Handicap* 1891), in which a cheroot-smoking but devoted Burmese is abandoned by a callous Englishman who marries a more refined compatriot. The Burmese girl searches for him for months, and when

she finds him happily married, renounces her claims and retires heart-broken.

[29] Percival Spear, *The Nabobs* (New York: Galaxy 1964) 13.

[30] *Ibid*, 136.

[31] Rudyard Kipling, "Lispeth," (*Plain Tales From the Hills*), *Works* (New York: Collier n.d.) 271. Lispeth reappears in *Kim* as the Woman of Shamlegh.

[32] Rudyard Kipling, "Beyond the Pale", (*Plain Tales from the Hills*) *Works*, 339.

[33] Gilbert, 179.

[34] Rudyard Kipling, *Something of Myself* (New York, 1937), p.82.

[35] *Ibid.*, pp.3—4.

[36] Woodruff, II, 17. The derogatory term for an Indian, *wog*, derives from the first letters of "westernized oriental gentleman," or *babu*.

[37] Rudyard Kipling, *Kim* (New York: Dell, 1963), p.239.

[38] See, for example, "With the Main Guard" (*Soldiers Three*, 1888).

[39] Christmas Humphreys, *Buddhism* (London: Pelican, 1951), pp.189—190, describes Tibetan Buddhism, also called Lamaism, as "a mixture of the best and worst of Buddhism, and of much that lies between. At its best it is a noble part of the Mahayana—or a separate school within it—controlled by men of the highest calibre; at its worst . . . primitive Lamaism may be defined as a priestly mixture of Sivaite mysticism, magic and Indo-Tibetan demonolatry, overlaid with a thin varnish of Mahayana Buddhism."

[40] It is not clear why the Lama does not educate Kim in a lamasery, or why he begs for his sustenance and then spends nine hundred rupees on school fees.

[41] Jullaludin McIntosh in "To Be Filed For Reference" (*Plain Tales From the Hills*, 1888) is Kipling's warning about what happens to a white man when he "goes native altogether."

[42] Rudyard Kipling, "Miss Youghal's Sais," *Plain Tales From the Hills, Works*, p.281. Strickland, also a master of disguise, languages and native customs, is a forerunner of Kim. He abandons his native ways and becomes "respectable" when he marries Miss Youghal, just as Kim does when he goes to school.

[43] The British had recently fought the Russians in the Crimean War of 1854—56.

II E. M. Forster

[1]Archibald Thornton, *The Imperial Idea and Its Enemies* (London 1959) xi.

[2]D.H. Lawrence, *Selected Letters* (London: Penguin 1954) 149.

[3]Leonard Woolf, *Growing: An Autobiography of the Years 1904—1911* (New York 1961) 135.

[4]Rudyard Kipling, "On the City Wall", *Works* (New York: Collier n.d.) 940.

[5]E. M. Forster, *A Passage to India* (New York 1924) 164. See Kipling's "Beyond the Pale," *Works* 339: "A man should, whatever happens, keep his own caste, race and breed. Let the White go to the White and the Black to the Black."

[6]K. M. Panikkar, *Asia and Western Dominance*, 1498—1945 (London 1953) 153.

[7]Rudyard Kipling, *From Sea to Sea* (London 1919) I 253.

[8]E. M. Forster, *Two Cheers for Democracy* (New York: Harvest 1951) 74—75.

[9]Kipling, *Works* 933.

[10]*Ibid* 407—408

[11]*Ibid* 407.

[12]E. M. Forster, "The Boy Who Never Grew Up", *The Daily Herald* (London), 9 June 1920, 7.

[13]Rudyard Kipling, *In the Vernacular: The English in India* (ed. Randall Jarrell) (New York: Anchor 1963) 105. Italics mine.

[14]Kipling, *From Sea to Sea*, I 165.

[15]*Ibid.* I 248—249. Kipling writes of the Chinese: "can anything be done to a people without nerves as without digestion, and if reports speak truly, without morals?"

[16]Rudyard Kipling, *Kim* (New York: Dell 1963) 55—56.

[17]Louis Snyder, ed., *The Imperialism Reader* (Princeton 1962) 271, quotes the London *Times'* correspondent's report of the Mutiny:

Some 200 prisoners . . . have been tried here (Peshawur), and we blew 40 of them away from our guns, in the presence of the whole Force, 3 days ago; a fearful but necessary example, which has struck terror into their souls . . . a prisoner bound to each gun, the signal given, and the salvo fired.

Such a scene I hope never again to witness—human trunks, legs, arms, etc., flying about in all directions. All met their fate with firmness. (4 Aug. 1857).

[18]Quoted in Malcolm Cowley, ed., "E. M. Forster," *Writers and*

Their Work: The Paris Review Interviews (New York: Compass 1961) 29. See also *The Hill of Devi* (New York 1953) 238.

19Rose Macaulay, *The Writings of E. M. Forster* (New York 1938) 188. Italics mine.

20K. W. Gransden, *E. M. Forster* (New York: Evergreen 1962) 85. Italics mine.

21Lionel Trilling, *E.M.Forster*(Norfolk, Conn. 1943), 150. Italics mine.

22E. M. Forster, "Reflections on India", *The Nation and Atheneum*, XXX (21 January 1922) 615. Forster writes in his journal (1921), later published as *The Hill of Devi*, 237, "the manners out here have improved wonderfully in the last eight years. Some people are frightened, others seem really to have undergone a change of heart."

23Forster, *Two Cheers*, 320. Martin Green is quite mistaken when he claims that *"A Passage to India* is 'out of time'—does it take place before or after the Great War?—surely no other intelligent book published in 1924, and so concerned with the modern mind, so completely ignores what had just happened to the world." ("British Decency", *KR* XXI (1959) 526—527.

24The Japanese victory over Russia in 1905, the Young Turk revolution of 1908—09, the Persian nationalist movement of 1910, and the Chinese revolution of 1911, all took place in Asia just before the war.

25Norman Palmer, "Indian Attitudes toward Colonialism", *The Idea of Colonialism* (ea. Robert Strauz-Hupé) (New York, 1958), 281.

26Louis Fischer, *Life of Lenin* (New York 1964) 526.

27Louis Snyder, *The Imperialism Reader* (Princeton 1962) 420.

28E. M. Forster, "India and the Turk", *The Nation and Atheneum*, XXXI (30 Sept. 1922) 845.

29E. M. Forster, *The Government of Egypt* (London 1921) 4n, 4.

30"E. M. Forster on His Life and Books", *Listener* LXI (1 Jan. 1959) 11.

31Quoted in K. Natwar-Singh, ed., *E. M. Forster: A Tribute, With Selections from His Writings on India* (New York 1964) xiii.

32Nirad Chaudhuri, "A Passage to and from India", *Encounter* II (June 1954) 19.

33Quoted and translated from Bengali (1873) by Nirad Chaudhuri "On Understanding the Hindus", *Encounter* XXIV (June 1965) 21.

34Forster, "Reflections on India", 614—615.

35Quoted in Archibald Thornton, *The Imperial Idea and Its Enemies* (London 1959) 306. Italics mine.

36Quoted in Arthur Koestler, *The Lotus and the Robot* (London 1960), 280.

[37] Sir Alan Burns, *In Defence of Colonies* (London 1957) 5.

[38] Quoted in Palmer 277.

[39] John Beer, *The Achievement of E. M. Forster* (London 1962) 135, is quite wrong when he says, "There is never any doubt that they [the Indians] need the justice and fair administration that the British give them," for the admirable Judge Das disproves this.

[40] Andrew Shonfield, "The Politics of Forster's India," *Encounter*, XXX (January 1968) 68, is entirely mistaken when he writes, "one gets the impression that Forster had little understanding and no sympathy for the complicated and courageous politics of the Indian independence movement".

[41] Aldous Huxley, "Wordsworth in the Tropics", *Collected Essays* (New York 1958) 2. Graham Greene writes of the Congo in *A Burnt-Out Case* (New York 1961) 63: "no one had ever walked under these trees lamenting lost love, nor had anyone listened to the silence and communed like a lake poet with his heart".

[42] K. M. Sen, *Hinduism* (London: Pelican 1961) 83.

[43] This passage also illustrates the opposition of two dominant symbols in the novel, water and snakes. Water, which symbolically stands between Adela and the "snake" as a protection, is associated with the Indians and the English characters sympathetic to them, like Mrs Moore, whose sense of cosmic kinship passed in and out of her like water through a tank. All water drains into the sacred Ganges. Water flows in the mosque tank when Aziz and Mrs Moore meet, and in Aziz's house in Mau where the torrent of hospitality gushed forth; and Aziz describes how, as a boy, he picked mangoes in the rain and emerged with water streaming over him. Water flows in Fielding's garden; and in the absolute silence after Godbole's song, no ripple disturbed the water. The Nawab Bahadur, an old geyser, expresses himself in streams of well-chosen words; and Mrs Moore is buried at sea, in the Indian Ocean. The rains come in the "Temple" section, from which the unsympathetic English are excluded, and which follows the hot and dry "Caves" section that is dominated by these English.

The snakes symbolize a principle of evil associated with the caves. Aziz warns Mrs Moore about snakes near the mosque and Ronny repeats the warning. Striking a match in the cave starts a little worm coiling and Mrs Moore associates the undying worm and the serpent of eternity. (The "undying worm" is a reference to Mark ix, 47—48: "And if thine eye offend thee, pluck it out: it is better for thee to enter into the kingdom of God with one eye than having two eyes to be cast into hellfire: Where the worm dieth not, and the fire is not quenched." See also *Paradise Lost* vi 739.)

[44]In "The Legacy of Samuel Butler", *Listener* XLVII (12 June 1952) 955, Forster admits that "Samuel Butler influenced me a great deal". He found the story of a human being who was worshipped as a deity in Butler's *Erewhon* for Forster writes, "witness the sad example of Mr Higgs, who escaped from Erewhon in a balloon and revisited that country to discover that he had founded a new religion and was being worshipped as a sun-god".

[45]Kipling, "Letters of Marque", *From Sea to Sea* I 99—102. See Psalms xlix.20: "Man that is in honour and understandeth not, is like the beasts that perish."

[46]Godbole's (pronounced God-bow-lay) doctrine of good-and-evil is not vague Hindu mysticism but a basic concept in western thought, and one quite familiar to Fielding. Milton writes in *Areopagitica:* "Good and evil we know in the field of this World grow up almost inseparably: and the knowledge of good is involved and interwoven with the knowledge of evil." (See Forster's "The Tercentenary of the *Areopagitica*", *Two Cheers* 51—55.) And Job ii. 10 asks, "shall we receive good at the hand of God, and shall we not receive evil?"

[47]Macaulay 193.

[48]Rudyard Kipling, "Egypt of the Magicians", *Letters of Travel, 1892—1913* (New York 1920) 274.

[49]Forster, *The Hill of Devi* 235.

[50]*Ibid,* 159.

[51]See Glen Allen, "Structure, Symbolism and Theme in *A Passage to India*", *PMLA* LXX (1955) 934—954, and V. A. Shahane, *E. M. Forster: A Reassessment* (Delhi 1962).

[52]Forster, *Abinger Harvest* 10. Godbole's love is not specifically Hindu or mystical, but religious in Forster's sense of the word. Cf. Mrs Moore: "God has put us on earth to love our neighbors and to show it" (51).

III. Joseph Conrad

[1]Georges Jean Aubry, *Joseph Conrad: Life and Letters* (Garden City, New York 1927) II 316 (14 July 1923).

[2]Joseph Conrad, *Lettres françaises,* (ed. Georges Jean Aubry) (Paris 1930) 87 (26 January 1908).

[3]Charles Carrington, *The Life of Rudyard Kipling* (New York 1955) 261n.

[4]*Joseph Conrad: Life and Letters,* I 208—209 (5 and 9 August 1897)

[5]Letter to Cunninghame Graham, 14 October 1899, *ibid.,* I 284.

[6]Ford Madox Ford, *Joseph Conrad: A Personal Remembrance*

(Boston 1924) 259–260.

7J. H. Retinger, *Conrad and His Contemporaries* (New York 1943) 124, 54.

8Conrad never wrote about Forster, but Forster's review of *Notes on Life and Letters* (1920), while criticizing Conrad for obscurity *in his essays*, praises him highly. Forster calls Conrad a "tremendous genius" and writes that his works are "interesting, stimulating, profound, beautiful", "Joseph Conrad: A Note", *Abinger Harvest*, (New York: Meridian 1955) 130.

9Joseph Conrad, "Heart of Darkness", *Three Great Tales* (New York: Modern Library. 1960) 271.

10Sigmund Freud, *Civilization and Its Discontents* (New York: Norton 1962), p.27n:
"No other technique for the conduct of life attaches the individual so firmly to reality as laying emphasis on work; for his work at least gives him a secure place in a portion of reality, in the human community."

11Joseph Conrad, *Nostromo* (New York: Signet 19 60) 396, 66.

12Blaise Pascal, *The Pensées*, (tr. J.M.Cohen) (London: Penguin 1961) 123, uses this same image to portray the human condition: ' Let us imagine a number of men in chains, and all condemned to death. Every day some are butchered before the eyes of the rest, and the survivors see their condition reflected in that of their fellows. Sorrowfully and hopelessly, all gaze at one another, awaiting their turn. This is an image of man's state."

13In his "Author's Note" to *Almayer's Folly* (New York: Signet 1965) vii–viii, Conrad writes of the Malayans, "there is a bond between us and that humanity so far away . . . . I am content to sympathize with common mortals, no matter where they live, in houses or in tents, in the streets under a fog, or in the forests."

14"Preface" to "The Nigger of the Narcissus." The theme of solidarity is particularly important in "The Nigger of the Narcissus," "Typhoon" and "The Shadow-Line."

15Quoted in Enid Starkie, *Arthur Rimbaud in Abyssinia* (Oxford 1937) 132.

16Henry David Thoreau, *Walden* (New York: Mentor 1956) 142–143.

17Carl Jung, "The Psychology of the Unconscious", *Collected Works*, VII (New York 1953) 18.

18Freud, *Civilization and Its Discontents* 26: "The feeling of happiness derived from the satisfaction of a wild instinctual impulse untamed by the ego is incomparably more intense than that derived from sating an instinct that has been tamed."

[19]Carl Jung, *The Undiscovered Self* (New York: Mentor 1957) 93.

[20]Joseph Conrad, *Chance* (London 1920) 390: "The normal alone can overcome the abnormal."

[21]Letter to his cousin Charles Zagórski from Freetown, Sierra Leone, 22 May 1890, in *Joseph Conrad: Life and Letters,* I 127.

[22]Conrad, *Lettres françaises* 61 (5 December 1903).

[23]*Letters of Joseph Conrad* to William Blackwood and David S. Meldrum, (ed. William Blackburn) (Durham, N.C. 1958), 154.

[24]This scene also provides a parallel to Marlow's farewell to his aunt early in the story, and a contrast to Kurtz's "savage and superb" native woman.

[25]Joseph Conrad, *Notes on Life and Letters* (London 1934) 156–157.

[26]This is very like Nostromo's feeling about "the San Tomé mine, which appeared to him hateful and immense, lording it by its vast wealth over the valour, the toil, the fidelity of the poor, over war and peace, over the labours of the town, the sea, and the campo" (400).

[27]Joseph Conrad, "The Secret Sharer", *The Shadow-Line and Other Tales* (New York: Anchor 1959) 123.

[28]In *Notes on Life and Letters* 294, 143, Conrad condemns "the modern blind trust in mere material and appliances" and affirms that "The true peace of the world . . . will be built on less perishable foundations than those of material interests."

[29]Joseph Conrad, *Under Western Eyes* (New York: New Directions 1958) 95.

[30]F. R. Leavis, *The Great Tradition* (New York: Gotham 1963) 194.

[31]It is impossible to agree with Robert Penn Warren who writes, "we must admit that the society at the end of the book is preferable to that at the beginning." Introduction to *Nostromo* (New York 1951) xxix.

IV. Joyce Cary

[1]Cary said of Conrad that "his books were a very powerful influence when I was a young man: his very strong sense of honour, his dignity, his whole moral sense, his whole approach to life. He was a powerful influence." (Nathan Cohen, "A Conversation with Joyce Cary", *Tamarack Review* III (1957) 13.) Cary describes Cock Jarvis, a character in the African sections of *Castle Corner* and the hero of the unfinished novel that bears his name, as "a Conrad character in a Kipling role". (Andrew Wright, "Joyce Cary's Unpublished Work", *London Magazine* V (January 1958) 38).

[2]Quoted in Andrew Wright, *Joyce Cary: A Preface to His Novels*

(New York 1959) 23–24.

³Joyce Cary, "Policy for Aid", *Confluence* IV (1955) 292.

⁴Joyce Cary *The Case for African Freedom* (New York 1964) 54.

⁵Aissa's name is taken from the wild Aissa in Conrad's *Outcast of the Islands* (1896), to whom Willems is fatally attracted, and who later shoots him.

⁶Kipling, "Song of the English". Bradgate is the DO in Aissa Saved.

⁷Joyce Cary, *An American Visitor* (New York 1963) 141.

⁸Other general parallels are Judy Coote and Fielding (she plays Adela's rdle in the plot but has many of Fielding's attitudes; like Fielding, she distinguishes between "Rimi" and "the Rimi people"), Burwash and Turton, Honeywood and Callendar, Doctor Schlemm and Mrs Moore, Mrs Pratt and Mrs Turton.

⁹But he is also insecure, socially awkward, easily influenced, a poor judge of character and prone to violence.

¹⁰Joyce Cary, *The African Witch* (New York 1963) 193–194.

¹¹Joyce Cary, Preface to *African Witch*, 313: "We must educate the Africans as fast as we can . . . . They want it at any cost . . . to satisfy need, to create some glory and dignity for themselves and those they love."

¹²Sir Hugh Clifford, the Governor-General of Nigeria, maintained in 1920, "the suggestion that there is, or can be in the visible future, such a thing as a 'West African Nation' is a manifest absurdity . . . . Any advancement or recognition of . . . these ridiculous claims and pretensions. . . is mischievous". Quoted in James Coleman, *Nigeria: Background to Nationalism* (Berkeley, 1958) 193. Cary takes an entirely different view in a letter of 4 October 1919: "Nothing endures forever. England will become little England again and Nigeria an Empire of the blacks— India of the browns." Quoted in M. M. Mahood, *Joyce Cary's Africa* (Boston 1965) 56.

¹³Frederick Lugard, *The Rise of Our East African Empire* (Edinburgh 1893), quoted in Louis Snyder, ed., *The Imperialism Reader* (Princeton 1962) 234:

The essential point in dealing with Africans is to establish a respect for the European. Upon this—the prestige of the white man—depends his influence, often his very existence, in Africa. If he shows by his surroundings, by his assumption of superiority, that he is far above the native, he will be respected, and his influence will be proportionate to the superiority he assumes . . . it is the greatest possible mistake to suppose that a European can acquire greater influence by adopting the mode of life of the

132

natives. In effect, it is to lower himself to their plane, instead of elevating them to his.

The wartime instructions given to British troops stationed in West Africa fifty years later are exactly the same:

> In all contact with the natives, let your first thought be the preservation of your own dignity. The natives are accustomed to dealing with very few white people and those they meet hold positions of authority. The British are looked up to, put on a very high level. Don't bring that level down by undue familiarity.

(The West African Review XIV (January 1943) 21; quoted in Coleman 152.)

[14]Salé later murders the Waziri and poisons the Emir to gain the throne.

[15]Despite Cary's disclaimer, the women's riots in the novel have much in common with the Aba riots in Nigeria in 1929, for an official report of the Aba riots was found among Cary's papers. Coleman writes (174):

> The rumor that women were to be taxed, and dissatisfaction over the abuses of native court members and warrant chiefs, precipitated a women's movement that spread like wildfire through two of the most densely populated provinces ot the Eastern Region at the end of 1929. Chiefs and Europeans were attacked indiscriminately and there was widespread destruction of property and goods, belonging mainly to trading firms. The riot was not quelled until the police, in an overwhelming show of force, killed fifty women and injured an equal number. An unusual feature was that the women, all illiterate, not only initiated but also were the only participants in the uprising. The whole affair was entirely spontaneous and received no support from either the men or the literate elements of the provinces. It revealed an amazing capacity for organization and united action which transcended clan and tribal boundaries.

[16]Letter of 10 September 1917, quoted in Mahood 40.

[17]Coleman 51.

[18]Coleman 165. The broken teapot given to the Emir by "gamna Gular" (Governor Lugard) is a symbol of the failure of indirect rule in Rimi.

[19]The central weakness of this novel (though not of others by Cary) is this simplified black and white opposition between African and English values, though Cary is also highly critical of English colonial administration. The other major fault is a serious lack of balance and

proportion. The sections on the polo and the bagatelle games are excessively long (cf. Forster's brief but highly effective polo scene, 57—58); and the episodes concerning Musa, Ibu and Fanta could be profitably deleted. The novel would gain considerably in focus and depth if the thirty-seven characters, many of whom are superfluous and often indistinguishable, were reduced by half.

20Philip Woodruff, *The Men Who Ruled India* (London 1965) II 26—27: in India in the 1860s there occurred the notorious incident "of a planter lashing out indiscriminately with a hunting-crop at a group of Indians; having paid to come on to a race-course, they had the effrontery to stand in a good place for the finish. That kind of thing would cause more bitterness than hangings."

21Joyce Cary, *Mister Johnson* (New York: Berkeley 1961) 155.

22W. R. Crocker, *Nigeria: A Critique of Colonial Administration* (London 1936) 207.

23Quoted in Coleman 145.

24Kenneth Kaunda, *Zambia Shall Be Free* (London 1962) 114.

25Joyce Cary, "Preface" to *Mister Johnson* 250—251.

26Joyce Cary, *The African Witch* 145.

27Mohandas Gandhi, *Autobiography* (Boston: Beacon 1959) 185.

28According to Gollup, "A chap may be a nigger — that's the way Gawd made 'em — same as 'e made warthogs and blue-faced baboons — 'e can't 'elp being a nigger" (134). Gollup is a typical Kipling sergeant, a worthy mate of the "Soldiers Three":

> You look at our battle honours, from Talavera to the Somme—
> there isn't a country in the world where we 'aven't laid down our
> lives for the Empire, and that's for you, Wog, for freedom—the
> Empire of the free where the sun of justice never sets (140).

Compare this with Kipling's "The Courting of Dinah Shadd," *Works* (New York: Collier n.d.) 805:

> They went to camps that were not of exercise and battles without
> umpires. Burmah, the Soudan, and the frontier,—fever and fight,—
> took them in their time.

29Quoted in Malcolm Cowley, ed., "Joyce Cary", *Writers at Work: The Paris Review Interviews* (New York: Compass 1964) 57. This is close to the social theme of *A Passage to India.*

V. Graham Greene
1*Letters of Joseph Conrad to Marguerite Poradowska, 1890—1920,* (ed. John Gee and Paul Sturm) (New Haven 1940) 12. The distance

from Boma to Leopoldville is nearly two hundred miles.

[2]Graham Greene, *Journey Without Maps* (New York: Compass 1961) 275.

[3]Quoted in James Coleman, *Nigeria: Background to Nationalism* (Berkeley 1958) 236.

[4]Greene was interviewed by the Leopoldville daily newspaper when he arrived in and departed from the Congo. In the first interview, "Graham Greene a séjourné à Léo dimanche," *Le Courrier d'Afrique*, 2 février 1959, 4, "Graham Greene a confié que le but de son voyage n'avait aucun rapport avec les récents événements survenus à Léopoldville et n'avait donc aucun but politique ou journalistique. 'En réalité,' a dit le célèbre romancier, 'je cherche le cadre pour un prochain 'roman-dialogue' dont l'action se passerait en Afrique. C'est donc en mission de reconnaissance que je vais séjourner à Coquilhatville.' " See also "Cinq minutes avec Graham Greene," *Le Courrier d'Afrique*, 9 mars 1959, 4.

[5]Graham Greene, *A Burnt-Out Case* (New York 1961) 49.

[6]Graham Greene, *The Heart of the Matter* (New York 1948) 8.

[7]Graham Greene, *The Lost Childhood* (New York: Compass 1962) 36.

[8]Graham Greene, *The Heart of the Matter* (New York 1948) 61.

[9]Graham Greene, *Brighton Rock* (New York: Compass 1956) 356. See also *The Lost Childhood* 77.

[10]T. S. Eliot, "Baudelaire", *Selected Essays, 1912—1932* (New York 1932) 343.

[11]Graham Greene, *The Power and the Glory* (New York: Compass 1958) 176.

[12]Quoted in Philip Stratford, *Faith and Fiction* (South Bend, Indiana, 1964) 237.

[13]Graham Greene, *The Lawless Roads (Another Mexico)* (London 1955) 5.

[14]Christopher Marlowe, *Doctor Faustus*, iii 80. *Paradise Lost*, iv 75.

[15]Greene quotes "The Love Song of J. Alfred Prufrock" in *Journey Without Maps* and attempts to draw a "hollow man" in *A Burnt-Out Case* and *The Potting Shed*.

[16]Graham Greene, *The End of the Affair* (New York: Compass 1958) 176.

[17]Graham Greene, *Three Plays* (London 1962) 138.

[18]Martin Shuttleworth and Simon Raven, "Graham Greene: The Art of Fiction", *Paris Review* III (1953) 31.

[19]Quoted in Marie-Beatrice Mesnet, *Graham Greene and the Heart of the Matter* (London 1954) 102.

[20]Mary McCarthy, "Sheep in Wolves' Clothing", *PR* XXIV (1957) 272.

[21]Quoted in Marcel Moré, "The Two Holocausts of Scobie", *Cross Currents* I (1951) 45.

[22]Letter from Graham Greene to Marcel Moré, quoted in Mesnet, 103–104.

[23]Quoted in John Atkins, *Graham Greene: A Biographical and Literary Study* (London 1957) 193.

[24]Greene, *Brighton Rock* 357. The spaced periods appear in Greene's sentence.

[25]Greene, *Three Plays* 69.

[26]Quoted in Guy Martin, "The Heart of the Graham Greene Matter", *Realités* CXLV (December 1962) 60.

[27]Despite temporary torment and fatigue Greene has continued to write prolifically. Since *A Burnt-Out Case* he has published *A Sense of Reality* (1963), a thin collection of four stories; *The Comedians* (1966), a book about the Duvalier régime in Haiti that is his weakest long novel; *May We Borrow Your Husband?* (1967), an uneven book of stories; *Travels with my Aunt* (1969), a humorous novel rather like *Our Man In Havana* and *A Sort of Life* (1971), an autobiography and the best of his recent books.

[28]Graham Greene, "Fiction", *Spectator* CL (10 February 1933) 194.

[29]Graham Greene, *In Search of a Character* (New York 1961) 31.

[30]Greene, "Remembering Mr. Jones", *The Lost Childhood* 99.

[31]Conrad's influence on Greene's other novels is also strong. *The Secret Agent* (1907) initiated the genre of the political mystery novel that was continued by Greene in *It's A Battlefield* (1934), *A Gun for Sale* (1936), and *The Confidential Agent* (1939). The Carlist theme of Conrad's *Arrow of Gold* (1917) also influenced Greene's suppressed novel *Rumour At Nightfall* (1931). Kurtz and Marlowe are characters in *The Name of Action* (1930).

[32]Fyodor Dostoyevsky, *The Brothers Karamazov* (New York: Modern Library 1943) 400.

[33]Joseph Conrad, *Victory* (New York 1924) 405, 410.

[34]Greene, *In Search of a Character* 26.

[35]Greene, *Journey Without Maps* 11.

[36]Graham Greene, "Three Travellers", *Spectator* CLXIII (8 December 1939) 838.

[37]The pouches under Rycker's eyes "were like purses that contained the smuggled memories of a disappointing life" (34). This detail is far too great for the object described; a writer more certain of his prose style would not embroider the simile so elaborately. Similarly, a man had to raise his voice at night" to counter the continuous chatter of the

insects, as in some monstrous factory where thousands of sewing-machines were being driven against time by myriads of needy seamstresses" (63). Though insects may sound like sewing-machines, the Zolaesque seamstresses carry us so far from the Congo that we have difficulty in following the next sentence.

[38]Greene deliberately exaggerates the horrors of the lepers in order to excite dramatically the morbid interest of his readers. I have spent some days at the leprosarium in Busia, Kenya, on the Uganda border. Most of the patients there were not seriously mutilated and their leprosy was barely noticeable except for slight discoloration and bumps on the skin. The leprous beggars on the streets of Nairobi and Kampala were far more horrifying.

[39]Joseph Conrad, "Heart of Darkness", *Three Great Tales* (New York: Modern Library 1960) 255.

Conclusion

[1]Quoted in Louis Nkosi, "Some Conversations With African Writers", *Africa Report* IX (July 1964) 20. In *No Longer at Ease* (1960) 106 and 39, Achebe refers to both Conrad and Greene.

[2]*Ibid.*, 19

[3]Chinua Achebe, *Things Fall Apart* (London 1958) 139.

[4]Quoted in James Coleman, *Nigeria: Background to Nationalism* (Berkeley 1958) 412.

[5]Chinua Achebe, *Arrow of God* (London 1964) 104—105, 286.

[6]Sir Alan Burns, *In Defence of Colonies* (London 1957) 42, claims that "the inhabitants of these [African] territories as a whole stood aside during the fighting and willingly accepted British rule. At its lowest assessment British rule was the lesser of two evils."

Josiah Kariuki, *Mau-Mau Detainee* (London: Penguin 1964) 48—49, expresses the modern African viewpoint, now generally accepted in the West, when he writes of Kenya: ' The Kikuyu rightly felt that their uneducated forefathers had not understood the nature and implications of the requests forced on them by the early administrators and settlers, nor had they the weapons or power to refuse any demand that was pressed really hard."

[7]Burns 67.

[8]*Ibid.* 23

[9]Graham Greene, *Journey Without Maps* (New York: Compass 1961) 69.

BIBLIOGRAPHY

I.   Works on Africa

Abrahams, Peter, *A Wreath for Udomo*, London: Faber 1956.

Achebe, Chinua, *Arrow of God*, London 1964.

Achebe, Chinua, *A Man of the People*, London 1966.

Achebe, Chinua, *No Longer at Ease*, London 1960.

Achebe, Chinua, *Things Fall Apart*, London 1958.

Assad, Thomas, *Three Victorian Travellers: Burton, Blunt, Doughty*, London 1964.

Beattie, James, *Bunyoro: An African Kingdom*, New York 1960.

Bellow, Saul, *Henderson, the Rain King*, London: Pan 1962.

Buchan, John, *Prester John*, London 1910.

Churchill, Winston, *My Early Life*, London 1930.

Conton, William, *The African*, New York: Signet 1960.

Coughlan, Robert, ed., *Tropical Africa*, New York 1962.

Dinesen, Isak, *Out of Africa*, New York 1937.

Ekwensi, Cyprian, *Burning Grass*, London, 1962.

Fagg, William, and Margaret Plass, *African Sculpture*, London 1964.

Forester, C. S., *The African Queen*, London 1935,

Gide, André, *Travels in the Congo*, New York 1930.

Gleason, Judith, *This Africa: Novels by West Africans in English and French*, Evanston, Ill. 1965.

Gordimer, Nadine, *The Soft Voice of the Serpent*, New York: Compass 1962.

Gordimer, Nadine, *A World of Strangers*, New York 1958.

Gunther, John, *Inside Africa*, New York 1955.

Haggard, Rider, *King Solomon's Mines*, New York: Collier 1962.

Haggard, Rider, *She*, New York: Collier 1962.

Hemingway, Ernest, *Green Hills of Africa*, New York 1935.

Hemingway, Ernest, *The Snows of Kilimanjaro and Other Stories*, New York 1955.

Howe, Suzanne, *Novels of Empire*, New York 1950.

Hughes, Langston, ed., *An African Treasury*, New York 1961.

Huxley, Elspeth, *The Flame Trees of Thika*, London 1959.

Huxley, Elspeth, *Red Strangers*, London 1939 .

Laye, Camara, *The Dark Child*, New York 1954.

Lessing, Doris, *African Stories*, London 1964.

Lessing, Doris, *The Grass is Singing*, London 1950.

Lessing, Doris, *This Was the Old Chief's Country*, London 1951.

Leuzinger, Elsy, *The Art of Africa*, New York 1960.

Mason, A. E. W., *Four Feathers*, London 1902.

Maugham, W. Somerset, *The Explorer*, London 1907.

Meyers, Jeffrey, "Culture and History in Achebe's *Things Fall Apart*", *Critique* XI (1968) 25-32.

Moore, Gerald, and Ulli Beier, *Modern Poetry From Africa*, London: Penguin 1963.

Moore, Gerald, *Seven African Writers*, London 1962.

Mphahlele, Ezekiel, *The African Image*, New York: Praeger 1962.

Ngugi, James, *Weep Not, Child*, London 1964.

Nzekwu, Onoura, *Wand of Noble Wood*, New York: Signet 196 3.

Paton, Alan, *Cry the Beloved Country*, London & New York 1948.

Ruark, Robert, *Something of Value*, New York 1955.

Sandison, Alan, *The Wheel of Empire*, London 1966.

Schreiner, Olive, *The Story of an African Farm*, New York: Modern Library 1927.

Schweitzer, Albert, *On the Edge of the Primeval Forest*, London 1961.

Segy, Ladislas, *African Sculpture*, New York 1958.

Segy, Ladislas, *African Sculpture Speaks*, New York 1952.

Shaw, G. B., *The Adventures of the Black Girl in Her Search for God*, London 1932.

Starkie, Enid, *Arthur Rimbaud in Abyssinia*, Oxford 1937.

Turnbull, Colin, *Forest People*, New York: Anchor 1961.

Turnbull, Colin, *The Lonely African*, New York: Anchor 1962.

Tutuola, Amos, *My Life in the Bush of Ghosts*, London: Faber 1954.

Tutuola, Amos, *The Palm-Wine Drinkard*, New York: Grove 1953.

Waugh, Evelyn, *Black Mischief*, London 1932.

Waugh, Evelyn, *Scoop*, London 1938.

Waugh, Evelyn, *They Were Still Dancing*, New York, 1932 .

Waugh, Evelyn, *A Tourist in Africa*, London 1960 .

Weyer, Edward, *Primitive Peoples Today*, New York: Anchor 1959.

Wren, P. C., *Beau Geste*, London 1925.

II.   Works on India
Anand, Mulk Raj, *Untouchable*, Bombay 1936.
Bates, H. E., *The Jacaranda Tree*, London 1949.
Burgess, Anthony, *The Long Day Wanes: A Malayan Trilogy*, London 1956—59.
Chand, Prem, *Godan*, (tr. from Hindi by Jai Ratan and P. Lal), Bombay 1936.
Chaudhuri, Nirad, *Autobiography of an Unknown Indian*, Bombay 1964.
Chaudhuri, Nirad, "On Understanding the Hindus", *Encounter* XXIV (July 1965) 2 0—33.
Gandhi, Mohandas, *Autobiography*, Boston: Beacon 1959.
Guillaume, Alfred, *Islam*, London: Pelican 1954.
Henty, G. A., *Through the Sikh War*, London 1893.
Huttenback, R. A., "G. A. Henty and the Imperial Stereotype," *HLQ* XXIX (1965) 63—75.
Koestler, Arthur, *The Lotus and the Robot*, London 1960.
Lewis, Oscar, *Village Life in Northern India*, Urbana, Ill. 1958.
Malgonkar, Manohar, *The Princes*, New York 1963.
Maugham, W. Somerset, *Stories of the East*, New York 1934.
Mehta, Ved, *Face to Face*, Bombay 1957.
Meyers, Jeffrey, "The Ethics of Responsibility: Orwell's *Burmese Days*," *University Review* xxv (Dec.1968) 83—87.
Michaux, Henri, *A Barbarian in Asia* New York 1949.
Naipaul, V. S., *An Area of Darkness*, London 1964.
Narayan, R. K., *The Financial Expert*, London 1952
Nehru, Jawaharlal, *Discovery of India*, London 1946.
Orwell, George, *Burmese Days*, London 1935.
Orwell, George, "Such, Such Were the Joys", "Shooting an Elephant", "Reflections on Gandhi", in *A Collection of Essays*, New York: Anchor 1954.
Rao, Raja, *The Serpent and the Rope*, New York 1963.
Sen, K. M., *Hinduism*, London: Pelican 1961.
Shils, Edward, *The Intellectual Between. Tradition and Modernity: The Indian Situation*, The Hague 1961.
Stephens, Ian, *Pakistan: Old Country—New Nation*, London 1964.
Wiser, William & Charlotte, *Behind Mud Walls*, Berkeley 1963.
Woolf, Leonard, *Growing: An Autobiography of the Years 1904—1911*, New York 1961.

140

III. Colonialism

Allport, Gordon, *The Nature of Prejudice*, Boston 1954.
Anene, Joseph, *Southern Nigeria in Transition, 1885—1906*, Cambridge 1966.
Arendt, Hannah, "The Imperialist Character," *Review of Politics XII* (July 1950) 303—320.
Bodelsen, Carl, *Studies in Mid-Victorian Imperialism*, London 1960.
Burns, Sir Alan, *History of Nigeria*, (6th ed.) London 1963.
Burns, Sir Alan, *In Defence of Colonies: British Colonial Territories in International Affairs*, London 1957.
Churchill, Winston, *India: Speeches and an Introduction*, London 1931.
Cohen, Sir Andrew, *British Policy in Changing Africa*, Evanston, Ill. 1952.
Coleman, James, *Nigeria: Background to Nationalism*, Berkeley 1958.
Crocker, Walter, *Nigeria: A Critique of British Colonial Administration*, London 1936.
Davidson, Basil, *The Lost Cities of Africa*, Boston 1959.
Easton, Stewart, *The Rise and Fall of Western Colonialism*, New York: Praeger 1964.
Fanon, Frantz, *A Dying Colonialism*, New York: Evergreen 1967.
Fanon, Frantz, *The Wretched of the Earth*, New York: Evergreen 1968.
Fletcher, Arnold, *Afghanistan: Highway of Conquest*, Ithaca N.Y. 1965.
Fyfe, Christopher, "The Legacy of Colonialism—Old Colony, New State", *Phylon XXV* (1964) 247—253.
Gopal, Sarvepalli, *British Policy in India, 1858—1905*, Cambridge 1965.
Graves, Robert, and Alan Hodge, *The Long Weekend: A Social History of Great Britain, 1918—1939*, New York: Norton 1963.
Hatch, John, *A History of Postwar Africa*, London 1965.
Heussler, Robert, *Yesterday's Rulers: The Making of the British Colonial Service*, New York 1963.
Hughes, Thomas, *Tom Brown's School Days*, London 1961..
Hutchins, Francis, *The Illusion of Permanence: British Imperialism in India*, Princeton 1967.
Jones-Quartey, K.A.B., *A Life of Azikiwe*, London: Penguin 1965.
Kariuki, Josiah, *Mau-Mau Detainee*, London: Penguin 1964.
Kaunda, Kenneth, *Zambia Shall Be Free*, London 1962.
Kenyatta, Jomo, *Facing Mount Kenya*, New York: Vintage 1962.
Magnus, Philip, *Kitchener: Portrait of an Imperialist*, London 1959.
Mannoni, O., *Prospero and Caliban: The Psychology of Colonization*, New York: Praeger 1964.
Masani, R. P., *Britain in India*, Bombay 1960.

Mason, Philip, *Prospero's Magic: Some Thoughts on Class and Race,* London 1962.

Mboya, Tom, *Freedom and After,* London 1963.

Moorehead, Alan, *The Blue Nile,* New York: Dell 1962.

Moorehead, Alan, *The White Nile,* New York: Dell 1960.

Newton, Arthur, *A Hundred Years of British Empire,* London 1940

Nkrumah, Kwame, *I Speak for Freedom: A Statement of African Ideology,* New York: Praeger 1961.

Oliver, Roland, and William Fagg, *A Short History of Africa,* London: Penguin 1962.

Palmer, Norman. "Indian Attitudes Toward Colonialism," *The Idea of Colonialism,* (ed. Robert Strauz-Hupé), New York 1958, 271-310.

Panikkar, K. M., *Asia and Western Dominance, 1498–1945,* London 1953.

Panikkar, K. M., *Common Sense About India,* New York 1960.

Pearce, Roy Harvey, *Savagism and Civilization,* Baltimore 1967.

Perham, Margery, *African Discovery,* Evanston, Ill. 1963.

Perham, Margery, *Native Administration in Nigeria,* Oxford 1937.

Reed, John R., *Old School Ties: The Public Schools in British Literature,* Syracuse 1964.

Robinson, Ronald and John Gallagher, *Africa and the Victorians: The Official Mind of Imperialism,* London 1961.

Runciman, Sir Steven, *The White Rajahs,* Cambridge 1960.

Segal, Ronald, *African Profiles,* London: Penguin 1963.

Shaw, G. B., "Preface" to *Misalliance,* London 1953.

Smith, Michael G., *Government in Zazzau,* Oxford 1960.

Snyder, Louis, ed., *The Imperialism Reader,* Princeton 1962

Spear, Percival, *A History of India,* vol.2, London: Pelican 1966.

Spear, Percival, *India: A Modern History,* Ann Arbor, Mich. 1961.

Spear, Percival, *The Nabobs,* New York: Galaxy 1964.

Strachey, John, *The End of Empire,* London 1957.

Thapar, Romila, *A History of India,* Vol.1, London: Pelican 1966.

Thornton, Archibald, *The Imperial Idea and Its Enemies: A Study in British Power,* London 1959.

Wilkinson, Rupert, *Gentlemanly Power: British Leadership and the Public School Tradition,* London 1964.

Woodruff, Philip (pseudonym of Philip Mason). *The Men Who Ruled India.* 2 vols. London 1965.

INDEX